To Mother:

with love

from Harry & Rose.

NEW ZEALAND
Land of many dreams

First published in Great Britain 1984 by Colour Library Books Ltd.
© 1984 Illustrations and text: Colour Library Books Ltd.,
    Guildford, Surrey, England.
Display and text filmsetting by Acesetters Ltd.,
    Richmond, Surrey, England.
Colour separations by Llovet, Barcelona, Spain.
Printed and bound in Barcelona, Spain.
by JISA-RIEUSSET and EUROBINDER.
ISBN 0-86283-166-0

NEW ZEALAND
Land of many dreams

Text by
James Duncan

Produced by
TED SMART and DAVID GIBBON

COLOUR LIBRARY BOOKS

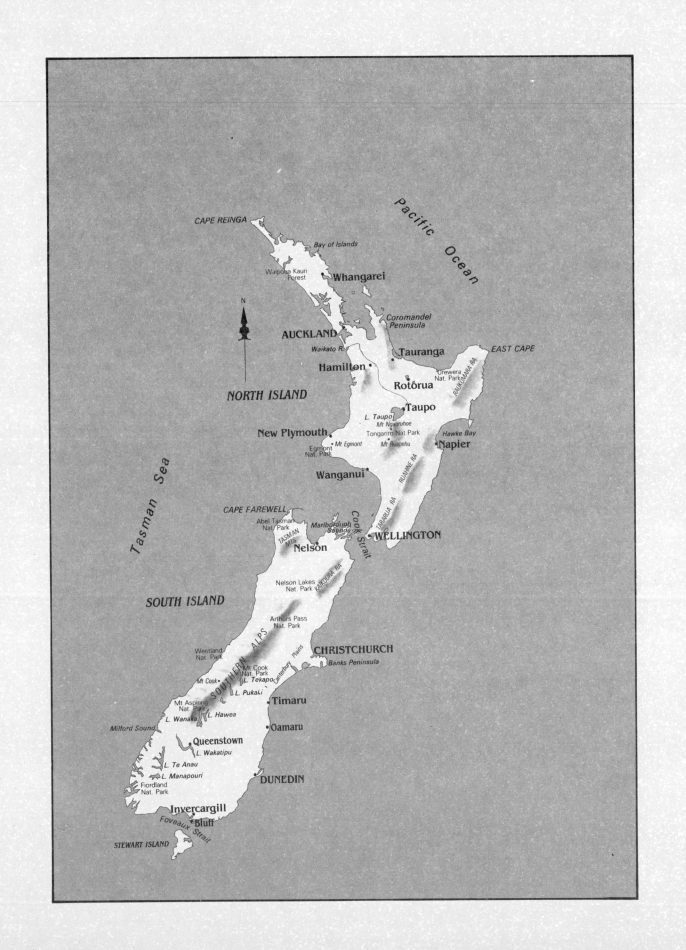

NEW ZEALAND LAND OF MANY DREAMS

New Zealand is a young land with perhaps the youngest human culture in the world. In the time since the world began, New Zealand's emergence from the sea accounts for only a couple of yesterdays and it was the last land to be discovered and settled. The impact on the landscape of the first race here, the Maori, was limited and only in the last 100 years or so has the arrival of Europeans substantially altered the primeval nature of the country.

The forces of planetary upheaval, which pushed up the mountain chains around which the New Zealand landmass has formed, are still at work. The lofty Southern Alps, the most conspicuous landform in the southwest Pacific area, have not yet finished growing. Volcanoes and hot springs are active in the North Island, testifying to the influence on New Zealand of warps and buckles in the earth's crust.

These signs of a young land still building have their counterpart in human society. The youth of the modern nation has given it a vigour to experiment with new ways of shaping society, earning it the description of "the birth place of the twentieth century" in the early 1900s. State experiment and social innovation were among the earliest traditions of New Zealand when Maori met the white man.

The land is the prime source of New Zealand's wealth. It is one of the most productive pastoral countries on earth and its industrial history is short, beginning in a significant way around World War II and broadening into major projects only in the last couple of decades. It is still mostly a country of forest and open farmland with high hills and higher mountains ever present in the background. Great natural beauty, small towns, modest cities, few people and an egalitarian democracy give it an air of unhurried prosperity. To say it has many elements of a South Seas paradise is not to overstate its virtues.

New Zealanders like to say that their country offers so much scenic variety that there is nothing to be seen anywhere in the world which cannot be seen here.

New Zealand's geographical isolation has strongly affected New Zealanders' view of themselves and their place in the world. There are big oceans to cross to reach any other land and with such a short history behind both Maori and pakeha we are inclined to look back to other places in trying to determine what has shaped us as a people. The Maori look back to their ancestral Pacific homeland of Hawaiki, the pakeha mainly to Britain but also to other parts of Europe and the more recent immigrants from Polynesia to their own islands.

The Maori came here only around AD 700 and their old belief was that at death their spirits travelled to the northern tip of New Zealand, where from Cape Reinga they leaped into the sea to travel back to Hawaiki. This ancestral homeland is not exactly identifiable but the race which first made New Zealand its home is generally thought to have come from the islands of eastern Polynesia, the far reaches of a scattering of volcanic mountain tops extending across the South Pacific from Papua New Guinea to Easter Island.

This first great wave of migration to New Zealand was followed by a second, larger wave from Great Britain. It began in the early 1800s, reached a peak between the 1860s and 1920s and still continues at a reduced level. The impact of this colonising culture has been great. Pakeha New Zealanders have, since World War II, declared themselves more or less independent of the ties which bound them to the "old country" although there are still pockets of resistance, especially noticeable when patriotic sentiment flows on public occasions.

Part of the way by which New Zealanders have arrived at recognition of their place as a South Pacific nation has been the third great wave of migration. It has brought in the last two decades or so thousands of Pacific Islands people following the earlier Maori path.

As with the people from Britain, they have come seeking an economic improvement to their lives. Many are naturalised or natural New Zealanders now, but like all migrants they still live with one eye looking over their shoulders.

The way in which New Zealand works politically is one of the things which New Zealanders have hammered out for themselves in their own fashion. Slung low under the earth's waist, tilting down towards Antarctica, with nothing between but the cold southern ocean, New Zealand lies apart. Between here and Australia – that worn, old paving stone of time – lie 1,800 kilometres of empty ocean; to the east there is nothing until South America, some 8,000 kilometres away.

The South Pacific islands to the north are as distant as Australia. Having found New Zealand, the Maori were able, in the absence of any foreign influences at all, to develop a unique culture. The pakeha culture too has had to develop its own style, even though it has traditionally had strong links with Britain in race, language and empire.

It is no longer advisable to speak of New Zealand as "The Britain of the South". It was a title widely used until the Depression and World War II began to separate New Zealand and British patriotic sentiment – even now there is a South

British Insurance Company in New Zealand. Although it was never true, the phrase "more British than the British" was often applied to New Zealanders, more for journalese than reality. Christchurch gained a name for being "more English than England", particularly among overseas writers seeking instant labels.

There is a paradox in that fading sentiment. The great majority of English, Scots, Welsh and Irish who came to New Zealand came willingly to escape the conditions of life in Britain. They were glad to be rid of the old country. But their sudden discovery here of geographic isolation had a powerful impact on them.

As R.A.K. Mason wrote in *Sonnet of Brotherhood*:

> "... what
> of these beleaguered victims this our race
> betrayed alike by Fate's gigantic plot
> here in this far-pitched perilous hostile place
> this solitary hard-assaulted spot
> fixed at the friendless outer edge of space".

Faced with the arduous job of obtaining land, clearing the forest, building roads, bridges and ports, housing themselves and generating an income from an almost virgin land, these British settlers who gave New Zealand its impetus towards modern nationhood cultivated a special relationship with Britain. Hard memories were overlaid with softer sentiments. It had no exact equivalent elsewhere in the British Empire.

There was a certain self-interest in the attitude. It gave New Zealand an emotional package in which to wrap its exports to Britain, for a long time our main market.

One New Zealand Prime Minister said New Zealand was tied to Britain not only through sentiment but also trade and debt. British investment flourished in a growing economy until the European Economic Community began to build an economic fortress of butter and cheese and meat, leaving New Zealand knocking politely on a closing gate.

A LAND ALONE

When the first Maori canoes arrived here, they found a land untouched by human hand, foot or tool since the beginning of the world. Elsewhere, civilisations had already arisen and fallen. Romans had conquered most of Britain hundreds of years before. While mankind struggled to form the earliest communities, New Zealand lay hidden. Australia was peopled by its Aborigines for thousands of years before the islands of New Zealand rose out of the sea before a wondering Maori navigator's eyes.

For millions of years since New Zealand had emerged from the sea, nature had been creating a place like no other. The land belonged to the birds, their kingdom the specialised forests.

The birds owed their supremacy to the great gulf which had opened up when the "New Zealand platform", as geologists have named it, swung away from the Australian-Asian and Antarctic landmasses about 70 million years ago. It had previously been joined to the southern super-continent of Gondwanaland, before it had begun to move apart some 150 million years ago.

New Zealand was cut off from other land long enough ago to miss out on the spread of people and mammals through the Australian-Asian lands. Without mammalian predators, New Zealand developed a remarkable bird life: birds nesting and living on the ground, birds living in burrows, birds using beak and claw to climb trees, birds so heavy they must launch themselves like a hang-glider to fly, birds which cannot fly at all, birds which graze on pasture, birds with different male and female beaks, birds with little fear of man.

In a climate which is generally moist and temperate, the absence of grazing mammals and of man allowed the land to grow enormous tracts of forest which could support myriad birds. Much of the New Zealand landscape was covered in true rainforest, particularly on the western slopes of mountains and ranges which catch the predominant westerly winds. The west coast of the South Island is renowned for its rainfall, which is heaviest over the fiords and mountains of the southwest corner.

Rainforest is the densest of all vegetation and to step off a track into the New Zealand "bush", a very generalised word for true forests, is to confront a tangled, thick curtain of ferns, creepers, vines and shrubs above which reach the giant native trees, festooned with climbers and epiphytes. Rotting logs, lichens and mosses, spongy carpets of leaves and other debris and the brilliant greens of the smaller plants thrust out a message of vigorous growth and competition.

Not all of New Zealand was so covered when the first men arrived. The tussock desertlands which are a feature of Otago and the central volcanic plateau of the North Island, the large areas of recent volcanic activity in both North and South Islands where scrub or tussock are common, were exceptions. But the New Zealand forest was then a marvel of specialisation which had very slowly developed over that long time since the land had begun a separate existence. Some seeds were common to New Zealand, South America and Australia during the time of Gondwanaland but some 2,500 of New Zealand's plant species are found nowhere else.

The vegetation of the lowlands is subtropical in type, while at higher elevations the plants become subantarctic in character, producing some beautiful and distinctive alpine flowers.

Four out of five New Zealand flowering plants are unique to this country and many kinds of plants are represented by only a single species, which underlines the distinctive garb which the great New Zealand forests assumed. This unique inheritance extends down to and under the coastal waters. New Zealand seaweeds differ in many instances from those in the rest of the world.

Beech forest clings to the eastern slopes of the high mountains, rainforest to the western slopes. The divide between them is sharp and positive. It reflects the way in which the cloud masses moving almost perpetually on to New Zealand from the west shed most of their water before they climb over the tops of the mountains and ranges.

The rainforest is distinguished by some magnificent trees. King among them is the kauri. No other tree can compare with it for sheer size, although it may not grow as tall as the rimu and kahikatea. The kauri is a pine tree, but it is to the northern hemisphere pine as a lighthouse to a candle. A dozen people linking hands around the base of one of the really big specimens might not be able to complete the circle.

Some kauri have contained as much timber as the giant redwoods of California. When mature, their trunks, marked by a pattern of bark that seems created by hammer blows, rise straight from the roots to crown, uninterrupted by side branches. The trunk does not taper at all. It has the symmetry of a pillar on the Parthenon. A lone giant or a grove of mature trees can be truly awesome. A tree like "Tane Mahuta", a prized example in the Waipoua forest sanctuary in Northland, has a mysterious power to express the stretch of ages. Such a vast tree standing so immovably among the quiet sounds of a forest, suggests a permanence which makes a human life span seem puny.

ANCIENT FOREST GIANTS

The oldest kauri are estimated to be some 2,000 years old. Trees now in their old age may have been cones lying on the forest floor about the time Caesar was invading Britain. Such a tree would have been in its youth when the death of Marcus Aurelius signalled the beginning of the decline of the Roman Empire. It would have been approaching middle age when the Vikings were starting their raids on Britain. Such a tree has outlived the Persian, Roman, Byzantine, Holy Roman and British Empires, as well as a string of Chinese dynasties.

Had Shelly seen such a tree as "Tane Mahuta", he may well have written not about Ozymandias but about *Agathis australis*, one of the world's most noble trees,

> "My name is Kauri, king of kings:
> Look on my works, ye Mighty, and despair!"

The kauri has the unusual habit, shared with several other New Zealand trees, of appearing quite different in juvenile and adult forms. It begins as a conical tree of great beauty, its slender but thick leaves producing a fresh and airy appearance. It can grow in this form for up to 100 years or so and makes an excellent garden specimen tree. But eventually the lower branches begin to fall off and as the tree attains its adult size it is left with a trunk rising sheer perhaps 30 metres above ground. The upper branches, sprouting like a tiara, and each as thick as a man, become a crest that might be a tribute from Tane, god and protector of the forest. Don't plant a kauri too close to your house if you're going to let it go its own majestic way – unless you want to live in a treetop.

The rimu is another tree which changes substantially between juvenile and adult form. After the kauri, the rimu has been New Zealand's most useful and widely used timber tree. When young it has long, drooping branches of pendulous leaves which weep more copiously than a willow. When it reaches its maximum height of about 30 metres, usually becoming the tallest in the rainforest, it too has a long, straight trunk but with a compact canopy.

The existence of some 200 flowering plants which change dramatically as they mature is a remarkable feature of New Zealand's flora. They bewildered early botanists.

New Zealand forest is generally evergreen and its colour tends towards olive green. Early pakeha settlers, anxious as all immigrants are to take something of their homeland with them, were quick to introduce elms, oaks, birches, willows and other trees which could be depended on to change into autumn colours and drop their leaves. Parts of the South Island can look especially brilliant with autumn colours and the effect on the landscape of wholesale forest removal and its replacement with foreign trees shows throughout the country when autumn arrives.

New Zealand plants do have some colourful varieties. No one who has ever spent a summer or Christmas in New Zealand fails to associate the period with the pohutukawa, a cliff-hugging plant of writhing, scaly limbs, grey and thick leaves and a gorgeous burst of brightest crimson in December. Pohutukawa, New Zealand's "Christmas tree", grow in long lines around the northern coasts, often draped over the cliffs as though nature's hands are protecting them from the sea. The rata tree, which grows among the forests in both main islands, also produces masses of scarlet blooms. Indeed, in the South Island the rata rivals the North Island pohutukawa for vivid display. You must cross west of the alpine divide to see it.

The golden kowhai, bearing masses of elongated flowers that might be birds clustering together for honey, has earned itself a place as a national symbol, usually seen in conjunction with the tui, one of the country's most splendid birds. The kaka beak, named after a native parrot, the korokia and its brilliant red berries, the makomako and its masses of tiny, creamy-white flowers, the titoki and its shiny black seeds cupped in a scarlet bloom, the many native herbs and the lush purple of the poroporo show that nature, looking back at the bush she had created, paused and threw down some colour before departing, giving the birds some decorative hues to live among.

In recent years, the New Zealanders' sense of identification with their own native forest, something impossible to see elsewhere on earth, has become stronger. Some of the most lively battles between environmental groups, government and business have been fought over the issue of native forest preservation. There has been a pronounced swing away from exotic to native trees for gardens and landscaping. Not everyone likes the New Zealand bush for ornament but more New Zealanders now find in the bush some reflection of their feelings as natives of the land. Perhaps of all the things in New Zealand, it is native bush and native birds which most appeal to the New Zealanders' sense of national belonging.

Other countries have the scenic features New Zealanders pride themselves on possessing; glaciers, mountains, lakes, volcanoes and hot springs. None has our bush and birds.

THE AXE BITES DEEP

It is little more than 200 years since the European axe first struck a kauri. Today, the kauri forests which once dominated large areas of the northern half of the North Island have shrunk to a fraction of their former size. There are pockets here and there, mainly on the western side of the long arm of Northland in Waipoua and Trounson Kauri Park sanctuaries. They are regenerating here and there but they are still being milled too. Forest parks on the Coromandel Peninsula and the Waitakere and Hunua Ranges near Auckland offer glimpses of these mighty trees.

But the size of the kauri was no match for the new age of steel which the pakeha brought to New Zealand. Neither, as it was to turn out, was the hard wood of the totara and rimu, the height of the kahikatea, the glossy beauty of the puriri and the scientific wonder of this whole plant world.

A Frenchman, Marion du Fresne, struck the pakeha's first blow against the forests of New Zealand on May 29, 1772. The sound of that first blow echoed and rolled through the trees for the next 150 years until the primeval rainforest had been swept away and grass grew in its place among the blackened tree stumps. It was an assault remarkable for its speed and extent. The main body of settlers began fire-storming the bush in the mid-19th century and within 60 years or so a country half covered in native forest had become two thirds introduced pasture and crops. A new economy set sail on seas of grass, sometimes moving briskly before fresh trade winds, sometimes wallowing badly in economic storms.

With the bush went the birds and the forest gods of the Maori. Tane, from whom the trees and birds gained life, fell back before a new economic order. By comparison with the tens of thousands of years it had taken nature to create the forest, its virtual destruction was over in an instant.

In *The Passing of the Forest*, W.P. Reeves wrote:

"The axe bites deep. The rushing fire streams bright;
Swift, beautiful and fierce it speaks for Man,
Nature's rough-handed foeman, keen to smite
And mar the loveliness of ages –
For Man's dominion – Beauty swept away."

The burning of the bush made a deep impression on the settlers, even though they had little choice if they were to build an economy out of the land. The bush was not all wantonly destroyed; for many years timber was New Zealand's main product and principal export.

It was an old kauri which du Fresne chopped down in the Bay of Islands. Perhaps the Maori gods were able to take some revenge – du Fresne was later killed and eaten when the Maori discovered he was a countryman of de Surville, the French explorer who had treated them brutally during his visit three years earlier.

Du Fresne could scarcely believe his eyes when he found in the Bay of Islands that one of the great war canoes, able to carry 100 warriors, was hollowed out of a single log. Looking at the hills around the bay, thickset with bush, he realised that here was a treasury of timber for ships' masts and spars. The British eventually became the biggest kauri buyers. Kauri also provided timber for most of the houses built in New Zealand during the first 50 years of intensive immigration. With beautiful grains and mottlings, honey-gold in colour and easily worked, kauri became a favourite furniture and decorative timber in New Zealand homes. It became the staple wood for boatbuilding as New Zealanders turned themselves into an enthusiastic sailing nation. Today, it is a prized timber and older furniture made of it sells at high prices.

An old kauri boat is today considered with the nostalgic respect *HMS Victory* or a New England whaler might command in Britain or the United States.

By the 1820s, ships were calling regularly at Northland harbours, Whangaroa, Hokianga and the Bay of Islands, to load timber. A Sydney firm opened a shipyard at Horeke, inside Hokianga Harbour, in 1826. The plunder had begun.

On his first visit to New Zealand in 1769, the British naval explorer Captain James Cook reported from Wellington's harbour that the dawn chorus of birds from the forest on the surrounding hills was loud enough to make shipboard conversation almost impossible. Visitors to New Zealand now look mostly in vain for glimpses of the New Zealand birds. Their place has been taken largely by blackbird, thrush, sparrow, mynah, starling and other imports, partly brought in to help control pasture insects. Native birds which can live with pastureland have done well but most needed the bush. Many have gone forever. Others are hovering on the edge of extinction and New Zealand now sadly holds one of the top places on the list of countries with the most wildlife species in danger.

Cook must have felt very much like the first Maori when he stepped ashore on New Zealand. He was beaten to New Zealand by the Dutch navigator, Abel Tasman, who in 1642, approaching the South Island from the west, saw "a great land uplifted high". He was the first white man to sight the Southern Alps and they must have appeared like magical towers; snowcapped mountains among seas which had previously shown him only flat lands and tiny islands under tropical and subtropical skies. Tasman did not stay long: the first European encounter with Maori in Tasman Bay ended when the Maori killed four Dutchmen who were attempting to make friendly overtures from a ship's boat to Maori in a canoe. He named the place Murderers Bay, which would sit oddly now on a place of golden sands and blue summers. We have therefore renamed it Tasman Bay.

THE COMING OF THE MAORI

Before Tasman and Cook was the semi-legendary Kupe, who according to tradition visited here in a canoe from Hawaiki and returned to his homeland to tell of Tiritiri o te Moana, Gift of the Sea. There followed a great migration and those first human dwellers would have marvelled at the richness and size of New Zealand after their small ancestral islands.

The Maori came in twin-hulled canoes and exactly how they found their destination is uncertain. It is hard to deny that they must have had considerable navigational skills, for by the time of European discovery there were perhaps 200,000 to 250,000 of them here, living mainly in the northern regions. Yet accident may have played a part too – when Europeans arrived the Maori knew nothing of Pacific geography. The story of a mass migration has been popular and the canoes of the so-called "great fleet" are important to Maori identity and tradition. From them the tribes took the beginnings of their genealogy in this new land Aotearoa: "Long Bright World" or "Land of Glowing Light", probably a reference to the brilliantly clear atmosphere which is a conspicuous visual feature of New Zealand.

There is no clear Maori tradition of a great fleet, although early white historians and myth-makers reckoned on such an event having happened in 1350. Goldie and Steel's painting *The Coming of the Maori* (borrowed from Géricault's *Raft of the Medusa*) was for many years accepted as the standard picture of how the Maori arrived.

With no written language, the Maori had to rely on oral tradition for their history. Invariably suppressing the history of defeated families and tribes, the lore which survived leaves much unknown and the other well-taught date of 925 for the arrival of Kupe cannot be definitely established from Maori learning. Modern archaeology suggests Maori were here at least a couple of hundred years earlier.

Although the Maori lacked the technology to make the impact on the land which the white man did subsequently, they did clear parts of the forest for their crops and took timber for their villages and canoes and they certainly caused the first human extinction of a bird species in New Zealand.

The earliest Maori have been called the moa hunters. Their culture was interwoven with this great flightless bird. Some species stood up to 3 metres tall. It disappeared well before Europeans arrived, killed off for food. The moa's value as a source of protein, available in a large economy size, made it irresistible to people living off a land without indigenous mammals. The Maori introduced their island rat, the kiore, and their dog, the kuri, to New Zealand and ate them, but the moa was at the top of the menu for the early Maori.

The moa hunters were able to herd the giant birds to a place of killing. They used its bones for decoration, its egg shell – as big as a rugby ball – to carry water. Even as a reconstructed skeleton in New Zealand museums, the moa is an impressive bird. There were some 27 different kinds of moa and 22 of them have been found in the middens and camp sites of their hunters. These moa hunters had a culture which was not entirely similar to that of the later Maori known to the earliest European visitors. Moa hunters may have been less warlike, as they seem to have lived in unfortified villages and their stone adzes were not fashioned as weapons.

During the 19th century, a myth developed among Europeans that before the Maori a race called the Moriori had lived in New Zealand and that the Maori had exterminated them. Modern research has banished the foundations of the myth but it is dying hard. It was a convenient belief for European settlers determined to take land from the Maori.

The Maori burned large areas of bush to drive the moa and then for their agriculture, but not until the British settlers arrived with axe, gun and plough did the threat of extinction extend to the majority of native bird life. Of the huge numbers of birds present in New Zealand before the pakeha settlers arrived, surprisingly few species have disappeared entirely. But many survive precariously and in much smaller habitats. Others have retreated to hill and mountain fastnesses as a tide of grass has eroded the forest line. Some exist only through the refuges provided by offshore islands. The Wildlife Service is engaged in several final-gamble breeding efforts for endangered species which are down to just a handful of survivors, and have been active in transferring birds to islands.

Of course the axe was not the only destroyer of the birds. Thoughtless shooting without regard for the future contributed. The koreke, or so-called native quail, was shot to extinction for the pot as its habitat of lowland tussock grass was burned off for pasture. Rats coming ashore from trading and immigrants' ships made immediate meals of eggs and young of many birds. Stoats and weasels introduced to control rabbits found easier meals in the birds. Dogs and cats gone wild found ground-dwelling birds easy prey. Introduced deer and goats helped destroy protective forest undergrowth.

The kiwi, one of the most famous of all birds and a national symbol, has suffered badly from the disappearance of forest and scrub. While still surviving in quite large numbers, its habitat is much restricted. Annual scrub burnoffs and general forest clearance are killing hundreds of these vulnerable birds.

Perhaps the saddest loss was the huia. Judging by recent interviews with people who remembered this bird, even those who knew that the forests had to be destroyed to make way for pasture were saddened by the passing of the huia.

Nothing else in creation was like it. A little bigger than a blackbird, the male and female huia developed different beaks. The male had a short, curved bill of normal proportion but the female had a slender bill more than twice as long. They worked in a special partnership to feed on the grubs which were their favourite diet. The male used his stronger beak to chisel and pull off rotten wood in which the grubs lived. The female used hers as a delicate probe within holes in the wood which her mate could not break off.

Such a special working relationship had social effects: it is recorded that a huia separated from its mate by death or capture would pine to death. The birds inhabited a limited area of bush in the Ruahine, Tararua and Rimutaka Ranges in the southern part of the North Island and fed almost exclusively on the huhu grub, the larva of a nocturnal beetle which infested decaying trees. Limited area and feeding habits made the huia sensitive to changes in the environment. It spent much of its time on the ground and was easily caught by hunters imitating its call and using a noose on the end of a stick. The Maori used its white-tipped tail feathers as a sign of mourning and for decoration. They honoured the bird by making beautifully-carved boxes, waka huia, solely to keep the feathers in. After the arrival of the Europeans the Maori helped to speed the extinction of the bird by supplying skins for commercial collectors and for popular 19th century mounted drawing-room specimens. The huia's lovely, flute-like notes, often sung in unison but a different key with a mate, was last heard around 1907.

It was New Zealand's most memorable forest bird and in a belated tribute it used to appear on New Zealand's sixpenny coin until decimal money was introduced in 1967.

MAKING A NEW LAND

The designs on New Zealand banknotes symbolise both the appearance of a new pastoral economy and the effects of it on the old forest and other bird habitats. Piwakawaka (fantail), titipounamu (rifleman), tui, kea and kereru (native pigeon) appear on our most common notes.

The use of birds on our symbols of wealth is an acknowledgement of the special place of birds in our environment. To the settlers who began arriving here in the mid-1800s, the environment had to be tamed. The bush was both a physical and psychological barrier to their progress. It was the domain of the Maori and their gods. The earliest photographs of New Zealand capture the enormous difficulty the bushmen faced in clearing rainforest from the up-and-down kind of landscape which forms most of New Zealand. The trees were huge. So hungry were the settlers for land that much of the bush was not logged for its splendid timber, but simply burned. In places it is still possible to see black monuments to the power of axe and fire. As B.E. Vaughan wrote around the end of the 19th century:

"The splinters stand on the hills,
In the paddocks the logs lie prone.
The prone logs never arise;
The erect ones never grow green,
Leaves never rustle, the birds went away with the Bush, –
There is no change, nothing stirs!"

Having fought a difficult, drawn-out war with the Maori, the swarming settlers must have seen the fall of the bush and sowing of grass as confirmation of their victory. As with the birds, so the bush retreat of the Maori shrank as civilisation's roads and farms advanced.

Out of the forest ashes New Zealanders created perhaps the world's most efficient and lush pastoral industry. Today, the grey-green of the bush in the hills contrasts with the brilliant greens of millions of hectares of grass which have made New Zealand the world's foremost agricultural trading nation for its size. Pioneering and using new techniques, New Zealand's farmers have been the economic backbone of the country for over a century. Industrialisation has been under way seriously since the 1940s but still agriculture accounts for half of this country's export earnings.

Today, New Zealand's rural face is fair, fresh and clean. High quality grassland farms rise and fall on the billowing green waves of the North Island where most of the beef and dairy farming and much of the sheep farming is carried on. Sheep numbered in millions spread through the foothills and the "high country" around the towering mountains of the South Island. Crops and livestock make the plains of Canterbury a pastiche of differently-coloured rectangles.

When huge, All Black rugby players run on to the fields of their own country or of foreign lands, they are a powerful advertisement for the quality and quantity of food which this green paradise produces for itself and for millions of people around the world. Since its earliest days, this small nation has helped feed populations considerably greater that its own. Historically, Britain was the main export market but, since World War II, trade with Asia, Africa, Europe and North America has expanded dramatically.

How did New Zealand, with a mere three million people, not much bigger than Britain and only twice as large as the State of New York, come to be the world's leading exporter of meat and dairy produce, the second greatest exporter of wool and, more recently, a successful exporter of a wide range of fruit?

There are several answers. Hard work is probably the main one. Fair climate is another. But New Zealanders are also inventive, willing to think of new ways around problems, eager to embrace new technology, cooperatively-minded, well-educated and healthy.

The foundations of New Zealand's success as a meat exporter were laid by its development of meat freezing. New Zealand had been turned so rapidly into a country of grazing fat sheep and cattle that by the 1880s the farmers were producing more meat than they were able to sell in New Zealand.

The New Zealanders invented a new way of marketing meat which was the most significant single economic move in the country's history. Settler farmers in Otago and local engineers set up a small freezing plant at which sheep were killed and frozen in small batches and loaded on to the *Dunedin*, a steam-sailing ship with refrigeration fitted. She sailed in February, 1882, and arrived in London with a cargo of meat which traders at the Smithfield meat markets said was as fresh and good-looking as English mutton.

The success of the shipment transformed almost overnight the way New Zealand was farmed. Previously the South Island had been mainly sheep-raising country – the North Island not being so quickly settled because of its hillier nature and the large Maori population, whose resistance to white settlement slowed farm development and led to the New Zealand Wars.

In Britain, where the population was still expanding as a result of the Industrial Revolution, food consumption was increasing and the invention of refrigeration meant New Zealand could help meet that demand with meat, butter and cheese. Further, it meant that wool no longer had to be relied on as the main export earner. Wool growing is suited to big estates, which were the mark of the gentlemen "squatters" – runholders who had secured big properties in the South Island – but meat, cheese and butter can be produced profitably on smaller farms.

Smaller farms, too, were better suited to the rugged nature of the North Island. And at the same time as the *Dunedin* sailed, the increasing population of settlers were clamouring for their own land. Refrigeration enabled many of them to have it and produced many more jobs in the new freezing works. Later, as the North Island farms were brought in, refrigeration helped dairy products into overseas markets, most going to Britain.

Britain, in fact, became the principal export market for the outpouring of New Zealand produce from the late 19th century until the last few years. For most of that time Britain took around 80-90% of all that New Zealand could send and this trade helped strengthen the average New Zealander's emotional view of Britain as mother country.

New Zealand has a few very large sheep stations today but most New Zealand farms are of moderate size, although very much bigger than the smallholdings on which much of Europe's agriculture is based. And mostly they are beautiful farms, laden with grass, well kept, tidy and highly productive. The main enemy of such productive wealth have been the policies of overseas industrialised nations who keep their farmers happy on huge subsidies which have built new Alps of meat, butter and cheese; products which New Zealand farmers have traditionally claimed to be the world's most efficient at producing. The claim is a fair one, for New Zealand has managed to maintain its record as mainly a primary produce exporter by selling in markets located 20,000 kilometres away. Touring New Zealand is often like travelling alongside some kind of educational display of pastoral farming. In many parts of the North Island the beauty of farmland is enhanced by the dramatic steepness and ruggedness of the hill country.

FARMING FROM THE AIR

Grass does not naturally grow well in New Zealand. Its soils are suited more than anything else to the growing of its native forest and exotic trees. The climate is for the greater part of the year mild to warm and rainfall is abundant. Long, dry, hot spells of weather are not a distinguishing feature of New Zealand's weather patterns and dry periods of more than a few weeks can very rapidly run a farm down. Climate alone is not enough to ensure productivity especially as the soils of New Zealand are deficient in phosphates and other minerals.

Fertilising farmland to maintain grass growth is a basic practice for New Zealand farmers. That is not easy on the steep hills which mould most farms. If New Zealand's 266,000 square kilometres were flattened out to the gentle contours which characterise Britain and Europe or the wide-open spaces of Australia or the United States, they would increase New Zealand's area by almost 70%. Two thirds of New Zealand farmland is too steep to be worked by ordinary farm equipment. As natural soil fertility fell following the introduction of grassland farming, ways had to be found of redressing the balance.

New Zealanders responded to their environment as they had responded with frozen meat. They added the aeroplane to the inventory of farm equipment. On a reasonably good day almost anywhere in the country during spring and autumn, planes can be seen swooping low over the farmland, diving down over ridges, climbing up out of narrow gullies, circling

and landing on short strips like fighter aircraft practising for another film on World War II. Behind them streams a trail, like smoke from a crashing plane. In fact it's dry fertiliser, the giveaway sign of the New Zealand invention of aerial topdressing – spreading fertiliser from the air at high speed.

During the war, New Zealand produced some of the best pilots who flew for the Royal Air Force and the Royal New Zealand Air Force. Bomber pilots were able to switch in large number to multi-engined civilian airliners when the war ended but the single-engined fighter specialist found jobs more difficult – the bomber boys were always at the head of the queue.

The single-seater pilots found a different job for their quicksilver skills. When aerial topdressing experiments began just after World War II, New Zealand was able to draw on expert pilots who skimmed the hills in manoeuvres they had executed in the skies over Britain, Europe and the Pacific. Soon there were more airstrips in the country than the RAF had flown from – something like 12,000 of them. They are often sloped, sometimes steeply, to allow a quick stop uphill and a short takeoff downhill. Time is big money here and turnaround of the aircraft, loaded by a hopper fitted to the end of a crane, can be done in half a minute if the strip is steep, one and a half minutes if not.

Many kinds of aircraft have been used, from the World War II Grumman Avenger torpedo bomber, which the Royal New Zealand Air Force flew in postwar experiments, and string-and-fabric Tiger Moths to the Fletcher, a modern plane designed in America to New Zealand specifications and built here. The planes take as much hammering as a wartime carrier plane – carrying about three quarters of a tonne of superphosphate and making perhaps a hundred landings and takeoffs in a day's flying.

Not every mission is completed. The flying is hair-raising and requires tremendous skill. Power lines are the worst hazard. Part of the cost of this important contribution to New Zealand farming success has been paid in pilots' lives.

The grass of the North Island has been put to another use besides farming, one which has made New Zealand an outstanding supplier of quality bloodlines. The racehorses of New Zealand are among the world's best, building up race-winning muscle on the grass they feed on as colts. There have been some legendary New Zealand gallopers but Carbine and Phar Lap outrank all the others.

Carbine was bred in 1885 and raced mostly in Australia, winning 33 of 43 starts and being unplaced only once. Sold to an English breeder, Carbine sired a winner of the English

Derby who sired another Derby winner who sired yet another. Carbine can be traced in the pedigrees of more than one third of the world's thoroughbred racehorses. Australians are reticent with the truth on the origins of Carbine because they are sensitive about the success of New Zealanders on their racetracks.

Phar Lap was as legendary a horse in the 1930s as Carbine had been earlier. He was New Zealand bred and ran all his races in Australia before being taken to the United States, where he died in peculiar circumstances, poisoning as part of a gambling conspiracy being suspected.

The Melbourne Cup is Australia's richest race and known throughout the world. Both Australia and New Zealand come to a halt for the few minutes the cup takes to run; the Australians because they cannot keep their money away from the bookmakers and the New Zealanders because their horses have a habit of stealing the race from under Australia's nose. The Australians should not really worry about that because the annual yearling sales in New Zealand bring over Australian buyers in regiments. They know the grass is greener on the other side of the Tasman Sea. A large proportion of Australia's best horses have been bred in New Zealand.

FOOD FOR THE WORLD

Butter and cheese may not be as glamorous nor as beautiful as sleek thoroughbreds but New Zealand is the world's leading exporter of them. New Zealanders consume more dairy products per person than any other people on earth but that amounts to only a quarter of total production so there's plenty left for overseas buyers. Dairying is a farming industry and farmers are known for their sturdy independence, yet the dairy farmers of New Zealand have had no hesitation in applying collective principles to their work.

The symbols of this are scattered around the North Island in innumerable towns, villages, hamlets and crossroad settlements. They are the dairy factories, the "co-ops", on which the export efficiency of the dairy industry has very largely depended almost from the day it began. In 1903 more than half of the cheese and butter factories were co-operatively owned by the farmers, who brought in the factory and office management skills they had neither the time nor the inclination for. The co-operatives now own almost the whole dairy factory industry. Most of the early monuments to New Zealanders' enthusiasm for the collective approach have been abandoned, replaced by modern plants like the one which stands by the Auckland-Hamilton highway at Te Rapa. Owned by the New Zealand Co-operative Dairy Company, it takes in milk from the large Waikato dairying district.

Fully automated, the Te Rapa factory is the biggest in the world; four storeys of concrete and glass that might be a modern hotel, blasting milk skywards in huge evaporators to turn it into powder. This and other modern dairy factories show that New Zealanders have always caught hold of the latest technology to keep themselves ahead of the competition. They are descendants of the now derelict and grass-sprouting, small co-ops which formed the basis of the dairy farmers' early wealth. People called the farmers "cow cockies" then, but wealth has since made that term seem inadequate.

Taranaki was and is perhaps the most productive dairying area in the world and an abandoned dairy factory seems to appear every two or three kilometres on the roads which radiate like wheel spokes around the hub of Mt Egmont, the almost perfect scenic volcanic cone.

Having organised their collectives on a local scale, the New Zealand dairy farmers went further and, in 1922, joined with the government to form the New Zealand Dairy Board – collectivism on a national scale – to deal in international trade. It, and the New Zealand Meat Board, grew out of New Zealand's experience in trying to market its produce to best advantage during World War I. The nation found that it was more profitable to make deals on behalf of everyone than to let individual farmers, companies and co-ops go their own ways. "Orderly marketing" has ever since been a creed of New Zealand farmers and only recently have they passed to the Meat Board extra powers giving it all authority to negotiate prices on overseas markets. Pragmatic as always, New Zealanders on the land were prepared to compromise their belief in free enterprise for efficient marketing.

More recently, the New Zealand belief in centralism was extended to the fast-expanding and prosperous horticultural industry when a Kiwifruit Marketing Authority was established to licence those who were to be permitted to continue selling their produce on overseas markets. As with the dairy industry, strict control of standards was seen as essential if New Zealand's reputation for top quality food was not to be harmed. A country so heavily dependent on its agriculture for foreign currency earnings has found it easy to justify collectivism.

The development of the kiwifruit industry is a story in itself and a book has been written on it. Not only did the kiwifruit, whose name owes nothing to a kiwi's diet, open overseas eyes and mouths to a gourmet's delight; it also sparked off recognition that New Zealand's climate and soils could grow new kinds of fruit and that grassland farming was not the only option for the North Island. Since the 1920s and 1930s New Zealand has been known as an exporter of excellent pip and stone fruit (an Apple and Pear Marketing Board ensures orderly marketing in New Zealand and overseas), but the kiwifruit suggested New Zealand could well broaden its range of crops.

The furry kiwifruit is, in fact, the old-fashioned Chinese gooseberry, renamed and marketed with a good deal of skill and profit. Many years of experiment, much of it unproductive, was undertaken in New Zealand to develop a commercially reliable and satisfactory fruit. Now it brings awesomely high prices in Europe, its russet-brown skin and bright green interior perfectly suited to presentation of an exotic image. New Zealanders even get to eat it themselves, so well has the plant been bred.

Kiwifruit are grown overseas now but as with other produce, the New Zealand skill in getting the best out of the land will be hard to beat.

Much of the New Zealander's inventiveness has centred around primary produce. As much thought has gone into making the world's most efficient milking sheds as has gone into the design, say, of Scandinavian furniture. This explains why New Zealand furniture is, on the whole, about as elegant as a Scandinavian milking shed. The backroom boys of New Zealand are more likely to be in agricultural research institutes and agricultural universities than in the laboratories of manufacturing enterprises.

WEALTH FROM THE NEW FORESTS

The big business in crops for New Zealand is in the pine trees with which many areas are still being planted. Unfortunately for the native bush, growth of pines for timber, pulp and paper, is so fast that it can be treated almost as a cash crop and, indeed, many farmers have planted it as such on their steeper hillsides. Native forests are being felled at the rate of some 16,000 hectares a year and the pines which conservationists once felt would take pressure off the natural bush by producing profits elsewhere, are now themselves a serious threat to the survival of the original landscape.

Since the 1950s the exotic forests of New Zealand have fed a successful, technologically advanced pulp and paper industry; the single biggest development of secondary industry in New Zealand's history. Without extensive mineral deposits, with limited coal and natural gas but with ideal soil for trees, New Zealand has found its timber a perfect base for industrialisation. It has become a major exporter of finished paper, the pulp from which it is made and wood chips for making pulp.

It also makes for domestic and overseas markets a wide range

of building timber and modern wallboards made from compressed bits and pieces which would otherwise be burned as rubbish. Everything but the pine needles find a use.

The seeds of this large industry sprang from Californian soil. On a tiny peninsula at Monterey, California, grows the radiata pine. This is its only natural home and the trees there are protected. Occasionally a New Zealand visitor is taken to see this reserve of trees to show off their immense scientific value. After initial puzzlement at the fuss, incredulous recognition dawns. Back home there are thousands of millions of these trees.

The radiata pine was introduced to New Zealand in the 1850s for farm shelter belts. Today it is worth a fortune to New Zealand. In its native ground it takes around 80 years to mature but New Zealand's warm and moist climate reduces that period to 25 years or less. Large-scale plantings of this tree began in the 1920s, following experimental nurseries established by the government in 1896 as a prelude to establishing state exotic forests. Using unemployed workers to plant these forests during the Great Depression helped accelerate exotic afforestation, and between the two world wars pines took over more than 270,000 hectares of land, mainly on the North Island's central volcanic plateau where grassland farming was unsuited to the soil.

At Kaingaroa, near Rotorua, the government made a new forest covering more than 120,000 hectares, the largest man-made forest in the world. The commercial success of forestry in New Zealand has diminished the original concern about the massive deforestation of native bush and consequent soil erosion to which exotic plantings were intended as a counter. Now the Forest Service, a state department, is subsidising the removal of much native bush outside national parks and other state reserves to encourage wholesale conversion of both timber country and pasture land to pine forests. On the main state highway between Auckland and Wellington, the traveller drives for 70 kilometres between continuous pine forests. In winter mists, a Scandinavian or German could be excused for mistaking his location.

Another of New Zealand's scientific achievements was the invention of a process for preserving the softwood of radiata pine. Some New Zealand native hardwoods, like rimu and totara, are long-lasting, but native trees grow slowly – the kauri needs 150 years to reach milling size, and rimu, the most widely used native timber, 200 years. Pine matures in a small fraction of those times but softwood timber has little resistance to weathering. But on the hills and volcanic plains of the North Island were more pine trees than the pulp and paper industry could use. And they kept growing at an alarming rate. How to extend the use of the pines?

The Department of Scientific and Industrial Research found a way by making pine even more resistant to decay than the natural hardwoods. The process, made available to the timber industry, pumps minerals at high pressure into the cut timber, impregnating the fibres and enabling the highest grades of treated wood to survive in the ground for at least 30 years, and above for much longer periods. Such timber need not be painted throughout its life and today is the standard building timber.

Invention of the process gave pine a considerably wider market and markedly increased the value of all those thousands of hectares of tall timber. Treated pine is so durable that it has, to a large extent, replaced other materials used for landscaping. Timber in gardens has become a mark of New Zealand suburbs.

Products from the pulp and paper and timber industries provide New Zealand's fourth largest commodity export but its 6% share of the total is well below the 57% taken by meat, wool and dairy products. Its total export earnings are less than half those of tourism and many New Zealanders feel the further loss of native bush to pine plantations is too high a price to pay for foreign exchange; particularly, they add, when overseas tourists want to see the things which make New Zealand different, not the things they see in many countries of the northern hemisphere.

New Zealanders wring production out of their farmland as they wring satisfaction out of beating the world at rugby union or the Australians at rugby league. They have in the process become the most adventurous of all farmers. But they have not won their grass-fed gains without paying a price. More than three quarters of the country is subject to erosion which, if not checked, could see a major and long-term decline in the country's food-producing ability. Infertile and unstable soils have had to bear the force of a sustained drive to make them grow what they do not grow well naturally. Some rivers carry millions of tonnes of good soil to the sea every year.

The Waipoua River, which runs into the sea near Gisborne, carries one of the highest proportions of sediment of any river in the world – up to 30 million tonnes a day in an extreme flood. The signs left behind by the downpours which regularly hit the land are hilltops stripped bare of grass down to the subsoil and great runnels of mud flowing down the gullies and valleys into the hungry rapids of flooding rivers and streams. A tenth of the harbour estuary systems which support fish breeding are grossly polluted. Not all erosion can be attributed to man. A country which is geologically quite young and mainly steep is naturally susceptible to the eroding assaults of wind and water.

It has been natural for New Zealanders to win as much of the resources of the land as possible to build a 20th-century economy and the standard of living achieved by a small population, so far from world markets and restricted to so narrow a range of products, is a remarkable achievement. In the last decade, concern about the impact of man on the environment has become one of the notable features of public affairs and many organisations with large memberships have sprung up to put nature's case to politicians, industrialists and other developers.

The national monument to such massive erosion is the Tarndale Slip in Poverty Bay, a region so named by Captain Cook not because of the lack of sustenance there but because his attempts to obtain food from the Maori there were rebuffed. Since then Poverty Bay has become one of New Zealand's most productive areas. Much of it has been built on the soils washed down to flatlands by innumerable floods and the Tarndale Slip is one of the signposts pointing to the effects of overgrazing and destruction of native forest. It is 80 hectares of migrating hillside which has resisted all efforts to stop it. Local people regard it with a kind of guilty pride.

Nature made itself a switchback ride in contouring New Zealand. Mountains and hills make a sharp profile for New Zealand. The Canterbury Plains and a few other small areas are our only real claim to gentility of landscape. Everywhere else is inclined towards heaven, much of it steeply cut by fast rivers.

Dominating all are the Southern Alps; a 400-kilometre chain of sharp rock, snow and glaciers. In it are 19 mountains above 3,000 metres, a spiny backbone for the South Island and the finest sight in the South Pacific, especially when seen across the Canterbury Plains on a fine day. The height of this massif contrasts markedly with Australia's mountains, which at their highest reach only about 2,000 metres. Around the mountains are lakes carved by glaciers which drew back some 18,000 years ago and south of the Alps is the forest fastness of Fiordland, a wilderness of mountains, lakes and glacier-gouged fiords.

The main mountain ranges of the North Island run northeast-southwest as the Southern Alps do, reflecting upthrust of the earth's crust along a line where two of the crustal plates which carry the earth's landmasses meet. The 600-kilometre Alpine Fault of the South Island is a result of these two plates, which meet with unimaginable force, sliding horizontally against each other. It is comparable with the San Andreas Fault which runs through California. The Alpine Fault lies along the western face of the Southern Alps. Here the mountains rise much more sheerly than on the eastern flanks, shoved up by buckling of the New Zealand platform along the fault line.

When the pressure between the two sides of the fault overcomes frictional resistance, the land moves and earthquakes jolt the island. Horizontal displacement of the land on each side of the Alpine Fault so far is estimated at about 450 kilometres.

There are some lowland and gentle landscapes in New Zealand but more than three quarters of the country lies above 200 metres. Mountains and high hills influence weather, recreation, farming, forest conservation, rivers and quite a number of other things.

The South Island has the most overwhelming scenic splendour in New Zealand, simply because of the scale of its mountains, lakes and fiords. But if the South Island can boast more snow and ice, more alpine lakes, more rainforest and more grandeur, the North Island is the perfect complement and has some individual attractions of its own.

THE FIRES BELOW

New Zealand is widely known for its geysers, hot springs and volcanoes, and the North Island is their main domain. The mountain crown of the island lies on the central volcanic plateau, an elevated area built by boiling magma welling up from beneath the earth's crust. Its 25,000 square kilometres were built up over several million years by tens of thousands of cubic kilometres of molten rock. The plateau is crowned by three volcanoes, two of them active and one still growing. Tongariro is an old volcano which is pocked with a series of craters and still shows a little of the old fires which built it in an active red crater, hot springs, a sulphur lagoon, soda springs and brilliant, mineral-coloured blue and green lakes. Like a child nestling close to its mother, Ngauruhoe has grown up on the slopes of Tongariro and is New Zealand's most continuously active volcano. Its symmetrical cone has the classic volcanic shape.

Ngauruhoe has overtopped Tongariro and how high it will ultimately be is anyone's guess. Every few years since records began it has thrown out steam and ash. In 1949 and 1954 lava overflowed the crater, the second being the biggest lava eruption recorded in New Zealand. In 1974-75 Ngauruhoe gave a splendid display of fireworks, with fountaining lava and the ejection of thousands of red-hot lava bombs.

Highest of the North Island's volcanoes is Ruapehu, the most dominant feature of Tongariro National Park which covers these three mountains and two other volcanoes nearby.

Ruapehu's huge bulk makes it the most impressive sight in the North Island. Its summit crater is still active and occasionally boils over with hot mud. Equidistant from both Wellington and Auckland, Ruapehu is the skiing centre of the North Island, crowded with visitors from both cities throughout the season. Skiing, like all sport in New Zealand, is not a class preserve. Stockbrokers mingle with farmhands, shop assistants with solicitors and labourers with doctors on the slopes.

Skiing on a volcano has a certain flavour of skirting around the dragon's mouth in addition to the normal risk of breaking limbs. Notices warning people what to do if the mountain erupts are prominent and the Department of Scientific and Industrial Research maintains an automatic monitoring system for advance warning of eruption.

The latent forces of these volcanoes were tragically demonstrated when, in 1953, an avalanche of water, mud and rock from Ruapehu's hot crater lake swept down the Whangaehu River and devastated a rail bridge 60 kilometres away. The night express from Wellington to Auckland plunged into the river and 151 people were killed.

Rock and mud avalanches of this kind, known as lahars, are common to volcanic activity and Ruapehu is surrounded by mounds where the avalanches have come to rest. Lahars are also a feature of the western Taranaki landscape around Mt Egmont, the second highest mountain in the North Island and visible from Tongariro National Park on a clear day. This volcano has been dormant since about 1755. It too is a national park and, according to Maori legend, was once one of a larger group of mountains situated where Tongariro National Park now stands.

The story goes that Pihanga, a breast-shaped female mountain within the park, was fought over by four warrior mountains. Tongariro won and the defeated fled – Putauaki 150 kilometres to the northeast (also called Mt Edgecumbe now), Tauhara to the northern shore of Lake Taupo, where it looms over the modern resort town, and Taranaki to the western edge of the land, where he was named Egmont by Captain Cook.

Behind him Taranaki left a conspicuous sign of his going – he is said to have gouged out the Wanganui River with his hasty departure. Early European settlers in the district claimed that the Maori would not settle on the line between Tongariro and Taranaki for fear of the latter returning for a second go.

Mt Egmont is prized by New Zealanders as one of their scenic gems and it is compared with Fujiyama in Japan. Egmont often appears in association with advertisements for cheese and butter, a symbol for Taranaki's dairy industry, but its outline is not as perfect as Fujiyama's, a secondary peak having grown up on its side. All the same, Ruapehu (2,796 m), Egmont (2,518 m), Ngauruhoe (2,290 m) and Tongariro (1,948 m) give the North Island a volcanic majesty which allows it to hold up its head with respect against the higher mountains of the South Island.

The New Zealand National Parks system began here, 15 years after the United States established the world's first such park at Yellowstone. These mountains were sacred, tapu, to the early Maori. The Tuwharetoa people had special veneration for Tongariro and their story of how fire came to it is a remarkable mirror of geological truth. According to legend, Ngatoroirangi, high priest of the Arawa canoe which was one of the great canoes from which the Maori trace their geneology, climbed Tongariro to claim it. In the cold snow no Maori had seen before, he performed the rites necessary for taking possession of new land. When he began to freeze he called for the fire gods of Hawaiki to save him. They sent down from the Pacific a chain of fire which burst out at White Island, Rotorua, Tarawera and Taupo before spouting out of Tongariro's craters. Hundreds of years later, modern geologists confirmed that such a chain of fire accorded with tectonic plate knowledge of a weak zone along this band through which the earth can bubble.

The incident gave Tongariro its name – Ngatoroirangi calling out that the cold wind from the south was carrying him away (*tonga*: meaning south; *riro*: to carry away). A slave named Ngauruhoe was thrown by way of thanks into the crater of the peak which bears her name. Ruapehu's name has more prosaic origins, simply a hole (*rua*) which explodes (*pehu*).

The Tuwharetoa decided in 1887 to give Tongariro, Ngauruhoe and the northern half of Ruapehu to the nation, partly to prevent it being awarded to rival claimants who had sided with the pakeha in the New Zealand Wars of 1860-72. Later, the southern portion of Ruapehu was ceded to the Crown by the Ngati Uenuku. It was a far-sighted gift by Tuwharetoa and a decisive influence on the subsequent development of National Parks in New Zealand. Pakeha had learned from Maori something about the spiritual value of the land.

NATURE SHOWS HER TEMPER

Volcanic steam and fire emerge elsewhere near this region. The mountains of Tongariro National Park are at the southern end of a chain of volcanic and thermal breakthrough which stretches more than 1,600 kilometres across the Pacific from the volcanoes of Tonga and the Kermadec Islands. Close to the park is Lake Taupo, the country's largest lake and site of perhaps the most gigantic explosion of all time. About 330,000 years ago a series of eruptions blew an enormous amount of material out of the earth and consequent slumping of the ground formed the lake bed. The size of the lake, 40 kilometres long, 30 kilometres wide and covering an area of 600 square kilometres, shows the scale of those big bangs.

All New Zealand's active volcanoes, geysers and boiling springs lie within a narrow zone stretching from Ruapehu to White Island, an erupting, boiling, sulphurous and dangerous volcano top in the Bay of Plenty. The beautiful, small lakes of the Rotorua district, the "thermal wonderland" which New Zealand tourism has promoted strongly for 100 years, were formed by volcanic action. The Whakarewarewa geysers, hot pools, boiling mud and mineral-laden springs at Rotorua give visitors a close-up of the hot earth, although steam draw-off from the surrounding area for heating Rotorua's homes, offices and hotels and for supplying private and public hot swimming pools is reducing the natural thermal displays.

The Waimangu thermal area south of Rotorua is more interesting for its undeveloped surroundings. It's near Mt Tarawera, scene of another cataclysmic eruption in 1886. The top of the mountain blew off with a noise heard from the South Island and hundreds of kilometres out to sea. In Auckland, 200 kilometres away, people saw the flashes of the eruption in the sky and the noise was mistaken at first for naval guns off the coast. After the initial explosion and flash, a series of craters 15 kilometres long opened up along the mountain's ridge as a knife might cut along the backbone of a fish. The eruption lasted less than 24 hours and left 102 people dead and a layer of mud and ash up to 45 metres deep for kilometres around. It was the biggest eruption seen by man in New Zealand.

An "eighth wonder of the world" disappeared under the rain of debris. The pink and white terraces by Lake Rotomahana had been one of the sculptured miracles of nature, formed by two separate geysers whose flow of silica built up a series of stepped pools on the shore of Lake Rotomahana. They were quite unique and by the 1880s were a drawcard for wealthy overseas visitors. Cliffs on the shore of the lake still steam as a reminder of the Tarawera eruption.

North and northeast of Lake Taupo are great sheets of ignimbrite up to 100 metres thick, discharged by the ancient volcanic eruptions from the Taupo region to flow down the slopes of the land in a cloud of fire. The big Taupo eruption of AD 150 destroyed ancient forests of totara and silver pine and created a landscape of scrub. The forests have never returned. The tussocky "desert" east of Tongariro National Park has resulted from the constant burning of the bush by volcanic fire.

The volcanic ferment in this small area of New Zealand owes its existence to the Taupo Volcanic Zone between Ruapehu and White Island. The zone sits over the same junction between the Pacific and Indo-Australian plates of the earth's crust which has created the Alpine Fault of the South Island. Other faults continue under the North Island in the same general direction and have pushed up the ranges which run between Wellington and East Cape – the Tararua, Ruahine, Huiarau and Raukumara chains. A relief map of New Zealand shows how the faults have produced the main landform foundations running northeast-southwest.

Along the Alpine Fault the plates are sliding against each other but under the Taupo Volcanic Zone they meet head-on and the resulting heat and pressure softens the earth's crust and lets through the molten magma from below. It is estimated that the volcanic material which has emerged under the volcanic zone and solidified is up to 4,000 metres thick, a greater dimension than the height of the Southern Alps.

POWER FROM FIRE AND WATER

The power of underground heat in the Taupo volcanic zone has given New Zealanders a source of electricity. Along with the Italians, New Zealanders have become the world's foremost experts at tapping geothermal steam for electricity. The Wairakei thermal field near Taupo township has been developed into a supply system for an electricity generating plant which is the second largest in the world. Right alongside the main North Island highway, Wairakei is a fascinating sight for all who pass by. Huge concrete exhaust pipes bellow with ejecting steam but the real work goes on inside the big pipes which take the steam from bores to a power house on the bank of the Waikato River.

Of course we have paid a price – nothing from nature comes free. Wairakei, also called Geyser Valley, was once one of the most magnificent thermal areas on earth. Larger than famous Whakarewarewa, it had some unusual blowholes and geysers. Alas, they have dwindled to tame toys. New Zealand's wish for plentiful supplies of cheap electricity, one of its most notable economic attainments, has put man's tight grip on many areas of natural beauty and not all have absorbed it easily.

The Waikato River, which runs from Lake Taupo to the Tasman Sea south of Auckland and is New Zealand's longest, has been dammed in eight places, destroying most of its original wild river scenic value – but creating popular recreational lakes at the same time. One of those dams was built at Aratiatia, scene of the North Island's most violent rapids which, once seen, were never forgotten. Now they flow spasmodically under control of the hydro-electric system operators. Orakei-Korako, a beautiful thermal area on the Waikato, was mostly flooded by one of the dam lakes.

Reeves's "beauty swept away" continues to put a sharp edge to New Zealanders' taming of the land.

New Zealanders pride themselves on their hydro-electric development which has reached a high degree of technical accomplishment. The larger schemes are in the South Island, where the snow-fed rivers flowing to the east from the Southern Alps pour out huge volumes of water. Here, men and their machines are still at work installing more generating capacity.

Although the North Island, with its Waikato River, had nearly all of the early development of hydro-electricity, which dates back to 1888 in New Zealand, the South Island is overtaking it by harnessing the big rivers from the Southern Alps. The most imaginative scheme is in the upper basin of the Waitaki River. This lonely, rolling land in the lee of the Southern Alps, speckled by tussock, is today crossed by wide canals. Those channel water from Lakes Tekapo, Pukaki and Ohau to four local power stations, from which the water continues on to Lake Benmore to pass through the older power station there and so on into the Waitaki River, increasing the flow through stations further downstream.

Benmore is the largest river-fed hydro project in the country, its lake as large as Wellington's harbour, penned up behind a 92-metre earth dam which is the country's highest. Putting more water through it increases the value of investment in it – and the other older station on the Waitaki. This trick of channelling water across country to make better use of existing power stations by maximising river flow has been done on a smaller scale on the North Island's central volcanic plateau. Here, the Tongariro Power Development uses tunnels and canals to change the pattern of natural river flow from the National Park volcanoes and nearby ranges, to put more water into Lake Taupo and down the Waikato River.

Clean generation of cheap electricity by water power has been one of the important factors in the development of New Zealand's high standard of living. It gave factories low-cost power and it made New Zealanders among the highest users of electricity.

There has been an impact on recreational use of rivers from hydro-electric dams and efforts are now being made by conservation organisations to retain the few remaining wild rivers in their natural state.

The search for hydro-electric power has also reached into

Urewera National Park in the North Island. The last and largest stronghold of the native bush which once mantled the North Island is in Urewera National Park, southeast of Rotorua. The drive in from the north provides a fascinating contrast, first passing orderly ranks of pine trees in the Kaingaroa forest, then diving into the crowded, luxuriant rainforest of the park and finally coming to Lake Waikaremoana, one of the most beautiful of the North Island lakes and surrounded by tall native timber.

If the Waipoua kauri reserve in Northland can offer the splendour of the kauri as a main showpiece, Urewera National Park displays most of the bush which used to grow throughout the island. The kauri is quite absent; curiously it does not grow naturally south of where the northern peninsula widens out suddenly towards the island's western and eastern hips. Instead of the kauri there are rimu, tawa, rata, beech, matai, totara, kohekohe and pukatea, all lovely trees attended in their majesty by retinues of ferns, climbers and perchers. This is thick forest where the spirit of Tane flits through the trees like the piwakawaka, the dainty fantail, dancing its aerial ballet in pursuit of insects.

Waikaremoana, whose name means "rippling waters", opens up excellent views of the bush and, nearby, small Lake Waikareiti is one of the few in New Zealand which lies completely unspoiled inside virgin forest. Waikaremoana has lost some of its original beauty. Changes in lake levels caused by piping its water to feed power stations just outside the park boundary have partly spoiled the foreshore.

Much larger hydro-electric schemes have been built on South Island rivers but everything is likely to be larger in the South Island. New Zealanders like to say that their country has a greater diversity of scenic wonders than can be found in any other country of its size. It is difficult not to agree when, after the volcanoes, hot springs and green hills of the North Island, you discover the frozen tops of the Southern Alps and the fiords and lakes which lie about them.

LAND CARVED BY GLACIERS

The Southern Alps and other mountains of this island have given New Zealanders a magnificent setting for more National Parks. Since the Maori initiated the concept by gifting land to the nation at Tongariro, New Zealand has set aside 7% of its land for National Parks. The South Island has seven National Parks which have a grandeur all their own.

The precipitous nature of the South Island's mountain chains and the great depths of the main lakes owe much to the scouring of solid rock by glaciers during the Ice Age of the Pleistocene period around two million years ago. The

glaciers which used to cover large areas of the South Island have retreated, but they are still slowly shaving off mountain sides in the higher parts of the parks.

The Tasman Glacier in Mt Cook National Park, 24 kilometres long and one of the finest continuous ski runs in the world, is the country's largest. It flows down between nothing but rock and ice in a park which is more than a third covered by snow and glaciers.

But the most striking glaciers are in the neighbouring Westland National Park, on the other side of the main Alpine divide. As we have noted, the western face of the Southern Alps, thrust up by the Alpine Fault, is markedly steeper than east of the divide. On the western side the land rises abruptly from a narrow coastal shelf, climbing from near sea level to 3,500-metre peaks in just 15 horizontal kilometres.

This steepness has produced one of nature's stunning visions. When Tasman was sailing in towards the west coast of the South Island he missed it; so did Cook. It was left to a couple of humble seamen on a brig, the *Mary Louisa*, to become the first pakeha to sight an icy shimmer between the stern rifts and ridges of the Southern Alps.

Afterwards, they wrote in their log: "At noon, abreast of Mt Cook, close in shore, we could see distinctly that it was an immense field of ice, entirely filling up the valley formed by the spurs of the twin peaks and running far down into the low land. It was a pale green colour and appeared to be quite a mile in width..."

The seamen, Francis and Young, had discovered one of the two west coast glaciers, the Franz Josef and Fox, which, like cascading pendants, ornament the mountain sides of Westland National Park. By the early 1900s they were New Zealand's most visited tourist attractions, easily accessible by a few minutes drive from the main coastal road and a short walk on to the ice where the terminal-faces give birth to icy rivers. The river which flows from the Franz Josef Glacier was named the Waiho by the Maori. The word means "smoking waters" and describes the low, writhing mist caused by the glacial water condensing the warmer air above it.

There is a strange juxtaposition here of subtropical rainforest and buckled rivers of ice. This is no arctic waste but a place where the southern rata blooms red and where thick forests cover much of the land between snow and sea.

It is the steepness of the Alps which brings the glaciers down to only 300 metres above sea level and within striking distance of the forest. In few places do glaciers reach such a low altitude. They used to be lower – probably about two kilometres further down their valleys – when Francis and Young saw them. Climatic variations which affect the snow basins feeding them make glaciers advance and recede, and the Franz Josef and Fox Glaciers on the west coast respond faster to such variations than any others known because of their steep incline and the temperate air where they end. In one 18-month period in the 1960s, the cold toes of the Franz Josef (named for the Austro-Hungarian Emperor, by the Austrian geologist-explorer Sir Julius von Haast) advanced 350 metres, sometimes moving more than a metre and a half a day – express-train speed for a glacier.

The Fox Glacier is only 24 kilometres away from the Franz Josef by road, so there is no bar to walking on two glaciers in one day. The ease with which you can reach them is deceptive, because their tumbled ice is dangerous and to climb any distance up them requires proper skills and equipment.

In the last decade or so both glaciers have shrunk somewhat, each recession wounding local hearts. However, a succession of cold winters with heavy snowfalls on the mountains will quickly bring them forward. During the Ice Age both glaciers extended another 20 kilometres into the sea and, if another ice age occurs, local tourist interests can warm themselves with the knowledge that the glaciers will advance again with giant strides.

SHAPES OF PAST AGES

Visitors to the West Coast can see signs of the forces which have helped to shape New Zealand. From the air it's easy to pick out the bush-covered humps on the coastal plain where the glaciers once spat out the rock they had chewed off the sides of the mountains. These moraines mark various stages of glacier advance and retreat. Withdrawal leaves the humps behind and lakes fill hollows in and around them. Some are gigantic. The main road skirts one end of the most distinctive of them; the Waiho Loop, four kilometres north of Franz Josef township. It is a perfectly-shaped quarter circle left from an advance which ended some 11,000 years ago. The climb up Alex Knob, by Franz Josef, is memorable for the panorama of morainic landforms visible from the top.

Best seen from the air is the Alpine Fault, which runs close alongside the main road between Franz Josef and Fox. It is possible to see the effects of the slipping of the one side of the South Island against the other, both vertically and horizontally, just south of the Waikukupa River on the main highway. The road passes through blue-green rock exactly on the fault and the rock is shattered from the pressure of the earth's crustal plates coming together many kilometres beneath the land surface.

One other sign of vast forces at work is the banded rock called schist, from the Greek word *skhistos* (to split). The rock is formed of parallel bands which can be split into slices and you can see examples littering the valley floors and river beds in Westland National Park. The bands show up as darker and lighter stripes and were formed when sedimentary mud and sand on the ocean floor was buried deep in the earth and then folded by movement of the planet's crust, squeezed as you might squeeze a ball of folded paper but so hard that heat and pressure turned the sediment into rock. Mica and other flaky minerals form the bands and the rock has a characteristic shine on newly-split surfaces.

The layers of schist are visible on the glacier valley walls, where the ice has planed the rock almost smooth. The folding which took place was so complex that waves can be seen in small stones, while the folds may be 3-5 kilometres apart in the main landforms.

The coastal road to Westland's remarkable glaciers used to peter out further south at remote Jackson Bay, but in 1960 a new tourist highway was built, turning inland to follow the course of the Haast River and cross the Southern Alps divide at Haast Pass. This long-sought connection between Westland and Otago is a splendid scenic route, jinking between rivers and mountains, and passing through Mt Aspiring National Park, where the Southern Alps end, and between Lakes Wanaka and Hawea.

West coast weather sets this part of New Zealand apart from the rest of the country just as the Southern Alps do. What an Aucklander might consider to be a tropical storm is a passing shower to someone living around Franz Josef, and the merest sprinkling to the people who watch Milford Sound disappear under a blanket assault by rain. Milford Sound is the most northerly of the deep-sea fiords which reach into the forested, remote mountains of the southwest corner of the South Island. How they keep the rain gauge afloat is one of the minor mysteries of Milford Sound, which annually records the country's highest rainfall – upwards of 6,000 millimetres.

Fiordland is the largest National Park, more than 1,200,000 hectares of mountains and water and almost as big again as the combined areas of the other National Parks.

When the glaciers were at full power, they were busy in this part of New Zealand. In the North Island the volcanoes flared red while Ice Age glaciers crept over the South Island, carving their future memorials as they went.

They deepened the main valleys and left lakes behind them when they fell back after the Ice Age ended. Evidence of the scale of these old glaciers, much bigger than those surviving in Westland, is in some of the very large moraines which lie at the foot of the lakes. The casual visitor can easily mistake them for hill ranges.

REMOTE FIORDS, STRANGE BIRDS

In Fiordland the glaciers created what have been named locally as sounds but are fiords: very steep valleys hollowed out below sea level by the ice and then invaded by the sea as the glaciers withdrew up the valleys. A steep drop in the sea bottom at the entrance to a fiord, where once the glacier ice ended its deep digging, distinguishes a fiord from sounds, in which the sea has invaded and drowned a river valley system. The Marlborough Sounds in the northeastern corner of the South Island is a beautiful example of the latter.

The fiords are long, running inland for up to 32 kilometres. All have immensely high, sheer rock walls on which forest and scrub cling precariously – mountains rising straight out of the sea. Milford Sound has the world's highest sea cliffs, rising 1.5 kilometres above the sea and reaching almost a further half-kilometre down to the drowned valley floor. So sheer are the walls of this and the other sounds that it is not possible to find an anchorage even right alongside them – unless you have a line 500 metres long.

Long and slender, the shape of the fiords is duplicated in the lakes which reach into the main mountains from the eastern side of the park. They too were dug out by glaciers which flowed down from the mountains during the Ice Age. Water divides the park in such a way that mountains reflected in lakes and fiords are the constant companions of visitors to Fiordland.

Best known of the fiords is Milford Sound and the drive to it is one of the great scenic experiences. But before there was a road, there was a track. In the 1880s, New Zealanders who had explored Fiordland felt that it should be opened up to tourists and although there were 15 other named sounds, Milford was the prize most sought. In 1888, Quintin McKinnon found with E. Mitchell a route into Milford over the McKinnon Pass. This is the highest point on the track which was subsequently put through to the sound from the head of Lake Te Anau, on the inland side of the mountains which form the central massif of Fiordland National Park.

From the early 1890s the track into Milford Sound was known as "The Finest Walk in the World". It has not changed and it takes four days to walk it with guides of the Tourist Hotel Corporation, a government agency which has concentrated on opening up major hotels in the more isolated areas of New Zealand. The corporation also operates hotels at other main

tourist centres like the Bay of Islands, the Waitomo Caves, the Rotorua-Taupo volcanic area and Tongariro National Park – an unusual example of government enterprise helping bring income to private enterprise.

In organising guided parties to walk the Milford Track to its big, modern hotel at the sound, the Corporation must be the only hotel-owner in the world to invite guests not to ride but to walk to their accommodation.

Guided parties use overnight cabin accommodation on the track which the Corporation maintains. You can walk the track on your own, using other, less comfortable huts, but must apply for a track permit from the Chief Ranger of the Fiordland National Park Board at Te Anau, who requires details of tramping experience, fitness and equipment. The precaution shows the wild nature of the region and even during the November-April summer season when the track is open, torrential rain can raise rivers and streams to dangerous levels.

The track offers superb views of dramatic scenery throughout its 53-kilometre length. It includes the floor of forested Clinton Canyon, aptly-named for its wide, U-shaped bottom and steep mountain sides which are the classic mark of past glaciers, and a steep climb to the top of McKinnon Pass at 1,154 metres. One of the finest sights is of the Sutherland Falls, 580 metres high and the fourth highest in the world, leaping out of a lake high up on the edge of a vertical canyon wall.

Most visitors go by road into Milford Sound, the only fiord served directly by highway. Although the other fiords are of equal magnificence, the sheer difficulty of pushing roads through to them means that they still slumber in seclusion. It was difficult enough to build a road through to Milford Sound because the nearest point to which a road could be taken up the Eglinton Valley was on the other side of a razor-ridged divide.

In 1889, W.H. Homer and G. Barber discovered a saddle across the divide which gave access between the three glaciated valleys the road follows today. But the saddle was impossible to put a road over and Homer proposed a tunnel. In the 1800s the cost was considered too high but when the Great Depression arrived the idea was revived and by 1934 the road from Te Anau had reached Homer's saddle. The tunnel was begun in July 1935, stopped in 1942 for the duration of the war, restarted in 1951 and opened in 1953.

The road dives between the typical, steep canyon walls of old glacier action in following the Eglinton, Hollyford and, on the other side of the tunnel, Cleddau Rivers and is one of the country's finest engineering works. Sheer spectacle crowds the eye so much that it is difficult to estimate the scale of what is around you. Both approaches to the tunnel climb up to cirques – blind valley ends like enormous amphitheatres. Mountains around top 2,000 metres and the 1,420-metre tunnel's portals are 923 metres and 795 metres above sea level.

Mountain, lake, river, waterfall, forest and fiord within a day's easy drive to Milford Sound can scarcely be surpassed for impact. And, of course, at the sound is the world-famous view of Mitre Peak. From the Tourist Hotel Corporation's lawns the hanging Sinbad Gully lies to the left and within its shadows lives a rare creature.

Of all the strange birds nature has bred, the New Zealand kakapo may be counted among the strangest. It is a ground-dwelling parrot with the face of an owl, has strong wings yet is unable to fly, sleeps and nests in burrows under the ground or in hollow trees and logs and booms like a bittern. The kakapo used to be known by the Maori of many generations ago in both islands. Today, it is restricted to a small area of Fiordland by Milford Sound. Introduced stoats and rats may be the final arbiter of the bird's fate.

Fiordland's second claim to ornithological fame is the takahe, which, since the mid-19th century, seemed to become extinct on several occasions but has miraculously survived by the narrowest margin. Its rediscovery in 1948 aroused intense scientific excitement. News of the rediscovery flashed around the world and for months after the takahe became an ornithological pin-up. The general public's imagination in New Zealand was fired by the description of this bright blue and olive green bird; yet another of New Zealand's flightless wonders. The problem for the takahe's survival is that it has a very specialised feeding habitat; the alpine grasslands of the Southern Alps. It lives in a small area of the Murchison Mountains on the western side of Lake Te Anau, almost opposite the resort town of that name. The area is closed to the public.

As a grazing bird, it has suffered from competition by deer for the grasslands, which include tall snow tussock. A large bird, more than 40 centimetres high and of heavy build, it grazes by snipping off the mountain tussock with its very strong beak. Takahe are strongly territorial and a couple stay together for life, marking out and taking exclusive possession of their area. Attempts to breed the birds in captivity at the Mt Bruce Native Bird Reserve in the North Island have had limited success but the outlook for these survivors of distant ages is questionable.

TUSSLE FOR A LAKE

Fiordland National Park is the site of New Zealand's biggest single conservation battle. Two of the country's most beautiful southern lakes, Te Anau and Manapouri, lie on the eastern edge of the park and of the two, Manapouri (its original Maori name was Moturau: Lake of Many Islands) is the most glorious. Both are part of the string of southern lakes which the glaciers scooped out on the eastern side of the main mountain divide in the South Island.

The continuing quest for hydro-electric power, something which New Zealand has become expert in producing, brought the state's engineers and planners to Manapouri with a proposal to raise the lake and use it to generate electricity for an aluminium smelter at Bluff, on the southern coast. Manapouri's beauty is almost legendary, to most observers the most scenic lake in the country – high praise in New Zealand. Despite this, despite Manapouri being in a National Park, despite the "Save Manapouri" campaign which put a record number of signatures to a petition, the scheme went ahead and today is a tourist attraction in its own right.

But the lake was not raised. The government of the day and its advisers were undone on that point by the painful testimony of Lake Monowai, another glacier-formed, small lake in the park which was raised in 1920 for electricity generation. Its shoreline is a ghastly array of decaying tree stumps killed by the raised water. The impact of that on Manapouri – whose shores and islands are entirely covered with dense, native forest – would have been fatal to its scenic attraction. Hindsight now suggests that the damage to the tourist industry would in the long-term have cost more than the value of the power the scheme produces.

Nevertheless, the Manapouri hydro-electric scheme is an impressive engineering achievement, with a power house built in a cavern hollowed out of solid rock 200 metres underground and reached by a spiral road tunnelled down to it. Water from the lake drops almost vertically down to seven turbines producing 700 megawatts and a 10-kilometre tailrace then discharges the water through the mountains into Deep Cove in Doubtful Sound. The two bodies of fresh and sea water are only 10 kilometres apart and the sound is 200 metres below the lake surface, sufficient drop to drive powerful turbine generators.

A launch trip to the lake's West Arm, a descent into the powerhouse and a coach trip over Wilmot Pass, between lake and sound, combine the beauties of nature with the ingenuity of man and the trip is rightly popular.

Extravagances by nature are not confined in New Zealand to birds like the kakapo and takahe in Fiordland National Park. Forests and Alpine heights have some remarkable botanic treasures. As well as having in the kauri the world's largest pine tree, New Zealand also has the smallest, the pygmy pine, which is found in upland bogs. It grows to only about 9 centimetres across.

As a counterbalance to such miniaturisation, the Southern Alps have the biggest buttercup in the world, *Ranunculus lyallii*, a real giant which may measure more than 30 centimetres across its leaves. The flowers grow to a diameter of 7-8 centimetres on stalks as high as your knee or higher. The plant is known commonly as the Mt Cook lily but is a true buttercup unsurpassed for size or beauty elsewhere. Deer love to eat it. It is only to be found in the Alpine regions of Canterbury and Otago.

Another buttercup distinct from all others for its short, fleshy leaves, and probably the rarest buttercup living, is one found only in an area of Canterbury covering about a hectare. Daisies too take on remarkable form in New Zealand. One species which many botanists say is the noblest of them all, the so-called leather plant, offers flowers 5-12 centimetres across.

TROUBLE WITH ANIMALS

Enemies of them all, including the seedlings of our biggest trees, have been feral goats and animals brought here and liberated for sport or commercial purposes. Rod and gun sports are popular and the country has built itself a reputation for the finest trout fishing and deer shooting in the world. Fabled stories abound about trophies and bags. Besides the red deer imported from Scotland, wapiti were shipped from America and freed in Fiordland, thriving and becoming much sought by sportsmen.

All the heavy bush and the alpine grasslands of New Zealand are infested with other introduced animals, whose effects on an ecology made fragile by its specialisation in the absence of mammals, have been disastrous. It has taken many years for this lesson to drive home. Even quite recent National Parks Boards' booklets have extolled the fine sport available through liberated deer, chamois and thar. Hunters resist the lesson, but general environmental opinion has moved against these animals because of their destruction of the native vegetation and consequent erosion and destabilisation in ranges and mountains which are extremely steep and naturally subject to erosion.

The opossum, occasionally the darling plaything of urban dwellers who capture a baby from the bush, is the most widely spread and harmful of all introduced animals. It was brought to New Zealand last century for a fur breeding industry which failed and has since spread through the bush like wildfire. Today, the balance is being redressed because of the value of opossum skins for export. Goats and deer destroy the bush from the ground, the opossum from above. Together, the combination has much diminished the natural vigour of the bush and threatened rarer plants with extinction.

Extermination is now the policy of the National Parks Authority. Private shooting of deer is encouraged under permit and these efforts have been assisted by poisoning and, more recently, hunting by helicopter. Thousands of deer have been taken by gladiators who jump from helicopters and wrestle the animals to the ground like a rodeo professional, and by nets fired from helicopters. These animals end up as stock on the deer farms which have become a flourishing new grazing industry in New Zealand for meat and antler velvet. The meat mainly goes to West Germany, the velvet to the purveyors of virility and other mysterious remedies in Asia.

Deer meat exports began with straightforward shooting of wild animals from helicopters. Good operators could shoot and recover hundreds of carcasses in a day and so good were the returns that Wild West-type tactics broke out at times, with aerial helicopter-and-rifle dogfights. With the virtual extinction of the wild herds in sight, the farming of deer has replaced them as the main repository of dollars on dainty hoof. At present, the antler velvet is the most profitable part of the deer but as herds build up meat will increase in value.

Pig hunting can still be found in many places in New Zealand, where a special technique of killing them has been developed. You chase them on foot with dogs and when they have bailed up the animal, you go in with a knife and stab it in the heart. It's a kind of Sunday morning fitness class for backblock farmers.

Hares run in some places in the South Island, brought in for sport and the colonists' pot but riding to hounds has never really taken on in this country. The stoats and weasels introduced to control rabbits failed to do so and became pests themselves; a threat to bird life. The rabbits have been pretty well brought to their knees by poison since the days when whole hillsides became fluid with them in the evenings, but some pockets still exist.

Books are still written giving imported animals an honoured place in the New Zealand creation but they are hangovers now from a disappearing belief that if you didn't take possession of the land in the name of your motherland, it might take possession of you.

Recent years have seen a kind of national fondness develop for the South Island's high country sheep stations, an antidote perhaps to the town life which most New Zealanders now live. Up in the mountains though, men ride free, just wind and tall clouds for companions – and, of course, their dogs. And all.those sheep...many New Zealanders like to impress people overseas by ritually informing them that this country has a population of more than 60 million sheep, but only three million people.

HIGH COUNTRY ROMANCE

Every country needs its own romance, and the high country may be New Zealand's version of the Wild West, something on which to diet, besides mutton.

Most high country farming is in the green pastures of the North Island but there is higher pictorial drama in the annual musters by big sheep "stations" among the mountains of Marlborough, Canterbury and Otago. The legend of a good, hard man working in a difficult, untamed land has become a literary tradition for New Zealand and it is still being made in innumerable books. The first man to write a book called *High Country Straggle Muster with Rod, Pack and Gun* will make a fortune. Today, the thrip-thrip of helicopter blades can be heard up there, dropping off sheepdogs and then becoming a herding machine.

The demands the high country makes on men and horses has had another result in the shape of machinery. It's a result which has been used in the Himalayas by Everest's first conqueror, New Zealander Sir Edmund Hillary, and has revolutionised speedboat racing as well as providing a form of transport which has turned fast and shallow rivers into tourist highways.

This is the jet boat, another New Zealand invention, made by Bill Hamilton when, in 1952, he tried to find a better way of getting up to the higher parts of his own South Island alpine property. The rivers and streams which flow down out of the mountains are also direct ways of getting up into the mountains, but they are broken by rapids, shingle banks, shallows, sharp bends and rocks. How to get a boat up them without wrecking hull or propeller and to do it with sufficient power to overcome the speed of the water?

Jet propulsion was Hamilton's answer and he turned it into a multi-million dollar business for New Zealand, which exports the boats and earns money from the licensed manufacture of Hamilton jet boats in other countries. Hamilton's brainwave improved a tried idea which had been wanting. He used an engine and centrifugal pump to suck in water and expel it through a steerable nozzle above the boat's waterline instead of under the water as people tried before. Quick steering is achieved by swivelling the nozzle, free to move because it is out of the water. With such a unit a boat has no interruption to a smooth hull line and can skim along in as little as 100 millimetres of water.

On inland waterways there is nothing to beat a Hamilton jet. Travelling in one at speed in a narrow river canyon or across rippling shallows, which seem guaranteed to rip the hull off, has all the thrill of a roller coaster ride with spray and thump of water adding a different sensation. Tourists now find that jet boat rides in the rivers of the southern tourist lakes area of the South Island give them some of their most vivid memories of a visit to New Zealand. The operators drive the boats in the same way a rally driver would put a car through a bendy gravel road to make sure you know what it's all about.

The land has treated New Zealanders well, supporting them with productive grassland farming since modern nationhood. The incredible range of scenery in such a small country is a strong guarantee that the land will continue to treat us well, attracting more tourists from overseas.

DISCOVERY AND LEGEND

This steep and tumbled country still exercises a strong influence on New Zealanders. Adapted to western agriculture and forestry for a comparatively short time, it retains much of its untamed character from the time before man. We have the world's shortest history of European settlement and the Maori were latecomers too. Science suggests that if the age of earth is divided into a year, the human race would not appear until the evening of the last day of the year. In that case, the first foot to touch New Zealand would have made it just an instant before midnight struck.

The Europeans of the 19th century felt that they were making New Zealand's first history but the Maori had already stamped their possession on the land through myth, legend and tribal and family genealogy. Their possession and subsequent loss of much of it heavily influences New Zealand society today.

The Maori say that when the clouds are low over Aotearoa and rain and mist fade the hills and mountains, we are seeing Rangi, the sky, weep for his enforced parting from Papa, the earth.

From the beginning of the world, Rangi the father and Papa the mother lay close together, their children, the gods, squeezed uncomfortably between them. To cover Papa's nakedness, Rangi had placed on her plants and trees and life was created among the forests and in the seas and rivers. Daylight and space to stand upright and breathe freely came when the gods rebelled against their parents and Tane, fertiliser of all life on earth and the most powerful of the gods, managed to push them apart.

The upraising of Aotearoa came after Maui, half-man, half-god was born. Maui is one of the supreme demi-gods of Polynesia. Mischievous, strong, taught in all the ways of the birds and the fish and the forest by Tama who lived on the edge of the sky, Maui took his grandmother's magic jawbone for his most powerful weapon. With his brothers he snared the sun and beat it with the jawbone so that it has since travelled slowly instead of racing across the sky as it had before.

With his brothers, Maui went fishing. He forced them, frightened though they were, to paddle far away to the southern waters, then unknown and empty. He smeared blood from his own nose on the magic jawbone and hooked a mighty fish at the bottom of the ocean. It was the home of Tonganui, son of the seagod Tangaroa. Maui sang his chants, the line sang too with the strain and up came a bright, new shining land, flat and peaceful.

The brothers leaped from their canoe onto the land to claim it. They ran to and fro slashing it with their weapons to mark their territory and the great fish, agonised by their blows, tossed and arched and when it lay still it was no longer a flat land but broken into mountains and valleys. Te Ika a Maui, the Great Fish of Maui, remains as rough today and the map of the North Island shows Maui's fish hook still stuck in the fish – the long curve of the Hawkes Bay coastline, ending at the northern end with the point of the hook. The Maori call it Te Matua a Maui, the Fish Hook of Maui.

Maui made the long legs of the pukeko, the dark blue swamp hen, in thanks for fetching water for him quickly. These birds have spread with the development of agriculture and are a common sight from the roads of the North Island.

Maui obtained fire from Mahuika in the underworld by asking for her burning finger and toe nails. A failure in communication led to an argument, and a forest fire, which threatened the whole world and Maui called on his ancestral gods to douse the flames with a storm. To save her fire, Mahuika threw the last of it into the kaikomako, mahoe and totara trees, which safeguarded it until the arrival of humans, who learned to rub these timbers together for fire. During this adventure, Maui assumed the form of the kahu, the native harrier hawk, to escape the flames and the kahu is brown to this day where scorched by the fire.

GODS AND TAPU

There is a rich store of Maori legend, some of it tangled with Maori social history. Kupe the explorer, who is said to have discovered New Zealand after Maui had raised it from the sea, may or may not have been a historical figure.

The Maui legends show how close were gods and demons to the Maori. The priests, the tohunga, knew protective witchcraft. They could enlist the aid of Tawhiri and Whatitiri, gods of wind and rain, Tu, god of war, Tangaroa, god of the sea and Rongo, god of agriculture. Other tohunga gave their blessings to the work of carving, tattooing and canoe-building as Christian ministers bless the harvest or the launching of a ship. Of more grisly skill was the tohunga who would cut the heart from the first enemy killed in battle and offer it to the gods.

Tapu was the Maori's method of maintaining class privileges, protecting sacred places, maintaining customs and ensuring proper community health standards. It had scores of applications. Tapu, (tabu or taboo elsewhere) had the kind of spiritual power that Christians believe resides in a consecrated church. It was attached chiefly to possessions, to act as an invisible police force, to burial grounds, to the village gardens. Breaking the tapu invited sickness or death from the spirits. So strong was belief in it that, as in other cultures, tapu could kill by simple acceptance of its power.

Tapu is still used today, generally to put a fishing ban on waters where there has been a drowning. It is always announced in the news of such a death if Maori are involved or the death has occurred in traditional fishing grounds.

Maori society was complex. All the tribes, sometimes called nations, trace their descent back to the arrival of a canoe from Hawaiki. They each had their own part of the North Island where the great majority of Maori lived. Some small tribes inhabited the South Island but the warmer North Island was more attractive to people without cloth-making ability.

The tribes were individual "nations". They had sub-tribes, or hapu and the hapu were made up of whanau, so-called extended families which had a network of relations much broader than that of the European family. The integration of groups within the tribe gave Maori life a very strong communal base. Maori today still have a strong sense of family and tribal belonging.

The central focus of community life was the marae, the meeting place where all the male Maori had rights to speak on tribal matters. The marae is still the main focus of Maori community life and in recent years many have been established in cities and towns to help maintain Maori culture among the urban population.

The Maori ate large numbers of shellfish. They also fished with bone hooks and nets made from native flax. They caught birds in ingenious ways, snaring the fat native pigeon at water troughs placed in the miro tree. The pigeons fed on the miro berries, which made them thirsty and they fell victim to looped snares arranged on the troughs.

There was much mana in the successful cultivation of the kumara, the Pacific sweet potato which the Maori brought here together with the yam and taro. Their ability to grow these tropical vegetables in New Zealand was a notable agricultural achievement and it took hard work and care. Kumara was a staple food. A South American plant, it found its way to Polynesia by some unknown means and the Maori grew it further south than any other agriculture had previously managed.

When the Maori gather today for a feast, or hangi, traditionally cooked in an earth oven, kumara is a favourite item, along with shellfish, pork and potatoes.

Old Maori villages had special pits for the storage of kumara and the volcanic cones of Auckland and Northland are pitted with them. These cones, scattered about Auckland city, tell the story of long Maori occupation through the kumara pits, shellfish middens and also through the large-scale terracing which the Maori made for meeting and living areas. Terracing, done by the most primitive tools, was a back-breaking job and is common on old volcanoes throughout the northern part of New Zealand. Maungawhau (Mt Eden), Maungakiekie (One Tree Hill), and Maungarei (Mt Wellington) in Auckland are superb examples of Maori occupation. Incessant warfare made these hills, along with coastal headlands, the most desirable places to own.

A PASSION FOR WAR

War was a passion of the old-time Maori. They engaged in it with enthusiasm and with many of the elements of bravery, challenge and fair play which were supposed to characterise European chivalry. Every battle was fought at close quarters, hand-to-hand. The short striking club, the patu, was the common weapon. The taiaha, shaped like a blunt spear, was not thrown but used as a two-handed jabbing and clubbing weapon.

Why warfare was so continuous is not clear. It may have had to do with population growth and the demand for fertile soil. Whatever the original causes, the Maori way of life had plenty on which war could feed. Utu, a system for exacting reparations for wrongs, fed endlessly on itself.

As in medieval Europe, the pa was a place to retreat to from the surrounding, unfortified village, the kainga, when war parties approached. Parties which came in peace went through an elaborate ritual of challenge, answer and acceptance which is still practised today on formal occasions ranging from welcoming the Queen of England on to a marae, to opening a new Maori or other community facility.

Pallisading of the pa was done with stakes of manuka, the common scrub of New Zealand, and cunningly-placed trenches gave defenders successive positions to fall back on. The Maori were adept at trench warfare hundreds of years before the western powers found themselves bogged down in them during World War I. The British soldiers shipped here for the New Zealand Wars found Maori entrenchment a formidable obstacle.

But there was another, more creative side to the Maori than war and it produced exquisite examples of craft. They excelled in carving with laboriously-fashioned stone tools. The art of carving as a tribal, community practice fell away during the musket wars the Maori waged against each other in the early part of the 19th century, and the dissolution of the close-knit Maori society under the spread of European influence meant that it never revived on the same scale.

Maori carving reached its highest art in the decoration of buildings, especially the large meeting houses and storehouses, gateways and war canoes. Almost everything had its decoration and the old carvings which survive are a tribute to the skill and patience of the old-time Maori.

Of all the materials with which the Maori worked they prized greenstone most. The stone is nephrite, which is similar to jade, and its hardness and translucent beauty were accorded supernatural properties by the Maori. They mounted expeditions over the Southern Alps to the Westland rivers where big boulders of greenstone lay.

There are two types of greenstone. One is named pounamu (green) and the other tangiwai (sounding waters). Both are found only in the South Island, which the Maori called Te Wai Pounamu, the waters of greenstone. Pounamu is the harder type and was used for tools and weapons, while tangiwai was used more for ornaments. Pounamu adzes and chisels made the majority of Maori wood carvings.

The Maori chipped greenstone off large boulders with infinite care by hammering it with other hard rocks and shaped it with sandstone and water, achieving the most beautiful finishes. Hei-tiki, small carvings representing a stylised human form of spiritual significance and hung around the neck, are the best known of the greenstone ornaments but there are also lovingly-made patu and other weapons. Greenstone is still being made into ornaments in New Zealand, export of the raw stone being prohibited. Several greenstone factories make commercial pieces. On a higher level, modern craftsmen are exploring new forms for greenstone and their art still owes much to the old Maori's liking for writhing, curving shapes. That is a tribute to the sensitivity of the Maori in drawing out the most beautiful expression of greenstone's qualities. Pounamu and tangiwai acquire great depth of beauty when skilfully carved and can reach a high value. Some modern pieces are so delicate they will ring when tapped.

The colour of greenstone varies from the darkest green to almost white, often patterned by small flecks. Because of its important place in New Zealand's oldest culture, greenstone represents for many New Zealanders not only an extremely attractive gemstone but also something of special value to their natural heritage. Fine pieces of either old or modern work tell you, when you look into them, why the Maori made so many arduous, cold journeys across the Southern Alps to find greenstone.

A NATION'S BEGINNINGS

New Zealanders celebrate two main events in the development of their modern nation. The Treaty of Waitangi laid the foundations for the joining together of Maori and pakeha under the British flag, and 75 years later the storming of Gallipoli's beaches by New Zealand troops gave the young nation a new and deeper sense of identity.

The Treaty of Waitangi was signed by Captain Hobson, New Zealand's first Governor, and Maori chiefs on a hot summer day in 1840. It took place on a lawn overlooking the Bay of Islands by the Waitangi River on February 6. It was the most vital gathering ever of the Maori, who agreed, through the Treaty, to place themselves under the protection of Queen Victoria. They were persuaded to do so by the impact on their society of new European ways. European traders had introduced muskets which changed the scale of Maori warfare and led to some tribes being decimated. They also brought liquor. Some traders obtained Maori land through fair dealing but others through trickery. There was a growing demand by migrant settlers for land but many Maori were anxious not to sell more, knowing how much they had already surrendered and how often on paltry terms. The influence of chief and tohunga diminished as Maori customs declined. The British at home, influenced by strengthening Christian evangelism, were concerned about exploitation of

the Maori and although their government was not eager to gain yet another colony, it gave Hobson authority to negotiate New Zealand into the Empire if necessary.

There were honourable intentions on both sides about the Treaty but in the end the hunger of Europeans for land overcame them. The Crown had the sole right to buy land from the Maori and the early settler government came under heavy pressure from Europeans who wanted it.

As Maori resistance to selling land grew, so did the pakeha demand for it. War broke out in 1860 and was largely over by 1865, although some isolated fighting continued for a few years. The Maori called the war the "White Man's Anger". They soon showed what resourceful and brave fighters they were, both men and women.

They built temporary pa of trenches and earthworks and challenged the pakeha to meet them. So good were their fortifications that artillery bombardment did them little harm – a lesson the European nations learned again in World War I – and in the beginning the Maori had all the victories as they cut down soldiers who tried to storm the pa after bombardment had ceased. The British quickly adopted the Maori's own tactic by driving their own trenches to the pa and slowly the balance swung their way. The Maori could not overcome the habits formed by hundreds of years of challenge and combat around the pa and devised no guerilla tactics which might have helped them.

The British Imperial troops sent out here came to admire the quality of the Maori warriors and had sympathy for them. The settlers were more concerned with winning because they had more of a stake in the outcome. As war sputtered out, huge areas of Maori land were confiscated and this destroyed much of the Maori way of life, so dependent on the tribal affinity with land. Also, the Maori lost their ability to retain a place in the new agricultural economy. They had gone into flourishing and profitable farming of pigs, wheat, potatoes, maize and kumara. They even had their own flour mills and, in the 1850s, Bay of Plenty Maori were bringing their produce to Auckland with a fleet of 45 coastal ships and 900 canoes. Without their food production, the early pakeha would have found it much harder to establish themselves here.

Ironically, the Maori's industrious copying of pakeha ways eventually worked against them. They were doing well while the pakeha were stamping impatiently on the edges of the land. After the New Zealand Wars the plough which broke the soil also broke the Maori spirit. Their population fell alarmingly following dispossession of their land and English novelist Anthony Trollope was gloomy about their survival after visiting here in 1872. But the Maori was not beaten and, in the 1930s, the introduction of improved health and social welfare measures helped them to regain their place in a mixed-race nation.

Today, the Maori are more vigorously and confidently demonstrating their own cultural values and their sense of race than at any time in the last century and a half.

Many New Zealanders feel that the Maori's customs, arts, songs and different attitudes to life have contributed a good deal to the interest of New Zealand society as a whole. Without the Maori dimension, New Zealand would find it more difficult to claim features which distinguish it from the western traditions which the pakeha settlers brought with them. It is the Maori element of our society which usually most interests overseas visitors and a New Zealander who knows something of Maori culture and can sing one or two of their songs will often find he has a more receptive audience when overseas.

There is a widely held opinion that New Zealand became a modern nation on April 15, 1915. On that day New Zealand and Australian troops went ashore to start what ultimately became a disastrous campaign to win the Dardanelles from the Turks as part of the British war effort.

The action took place at Gallipoli and the Australian and New Zealand Army Corps, specially assembled for the invasion, earned immortality for their gallantry and tenacity. The shortened title of Anzac has become a synonym for New Zealand-Australian comradeship and a do-or-die fighting spirit. Anzac Day is marked every year by both countries and is our most patriotic day, a remembrance for the fallen not only in World Wars I and II but also in the Korean and Vietnam Wars.

The shock of the casualties at Gallipoli imprinted itself on people's minds as nothing had done before. Waitangi had been a significant event but Gallipoli had a sudden, jolting impact because of the degree of personal loss. New Zealand had only one million people in 1914 and nearly 17,000 men died at the Dardanelles and on other overseas battlefields. Total casualties numbered 58,000, or one out of every seventeen New Zealanders.

A STEP INTO NATIONHOOD

Gallipoli was seen as marking New Zealand's sudden initiation into full nationhood. A country which had been preoccupied with its internal development suddenly found itself drawn into the larger world outside. Yet before Gallipoli, New Zealand had already been forming a new and different kind of nation through political innovation. It may have been less dramatic than the charges of the Anzacs but it began to chart the kind of course New Zealanders wanted their nation to follow.

This new nation was by the late 1800s already well along the road to being a socially conscious state, a road followed by almost every developed nation since, long after the dust of New Zealand's pioneering ways had settled. In 1905, a visiting American professor called New Zealand "the birth place of the Twentieth Century" and wrote a book about it. Another American writer on socialism hoped, around the beginning of this century, that nations would guarantee "the nurture, education and comfortable maintenance of every citizen from the cradle to the grave". The last phrase has been used over and over again to refer to the New Zealand way of running government, either in a kindly or hostile sense. Bellamy was looking forward to the year 2000 but New Zealand was, by 1900, already taking many socialist initiatives. The pattern has continued and New Zealand has perhaps the most highly-organised systems of state ownership of public services and central welfare to exist under a fully democratic electoral system.

There is a common feeling that the state represents the people and that governments have a responsibility to ensure equal access to the common wealth.

The New Zealand search for equality was to a large extent a reaction against the class and property system of Great Britain. When it seemed that a wealthy, self-perpetuating government of big landowners was becoming established in New Zealand, the 1890 Liberal Government broke it up by compelling the division of large estates into the small farms which have been the basis of New Zealand wealth. The popularity of the government's move was accentuated by the long depression between 1879 and 1896. Depression and the Liberal Government together provided a sudden impetus towards the modern democratic state.

There were already in place some innovative democratic models which helped the process: free, compulsory and secular elementary education in 1877, a Government Life Insurance Office and Public Trust Office, the secret ballot in 1869, full adult male suffrage in 1879. The Liberals founded a Labour Department to oversee working conditions and in 1894 gave the world its first Industrial Conciliation and Arbitration Act, a compulsory system to gave the state a means of influencing industrial relations. In 1894, the government nationalised the Bank of New Zealand and, in 1898, New Zealand introduced the world's first comprehensive national old age pension scheme.

More radically, all adult women were given the vote in 1893. New Zealand was the first country to give women that right, responding to pressure from the Women's Christian Temperance Union, which saw in the vote a way of bringing in prohibition. They failed by a hair's breadth in a referendum immediately on the ending of World War II. Only the votes of soldiers overseas prevented it.

PEOPLE AND STATE

The Liberals established an important concept in New Zealand: people working together through the agency of the state. It has moulded the New Zealand attitude to politics and economics. As New Zealand historian Keith Sinclair has said, New Zealanders have shown little fear of the state and in general it has served them well.

Farmers went along with state measures enabling them to centralise control of shipping produce to Britain and marketing it there. The "producer boards" are an essential part of New Zealand farming strategy. When the Great Depression of the 1930s arrived, the impact of falling prices on farmers who had been established on the land by government resettlement programmes after World War I was an important factor in the election of the country's first Labour Government. From 1935 to 1949 successive Labour Governments expanded state influence, introducing for farmers guaranteed minimum prices subsidised when necessary from taxes, a basic minimum wage for all workers, new pension schemes, state housing for rental, state payments to parents to subsidise child-rearing costs and a national health service.

This approach has continued at varying pace under successive governments. Since World War II New Zealand has introduced a comprehensive accident compensation scheme which operates irrespective of fault. No longer are court cases necessary to win compensation and even injuries from recreation and sport are covered. It was hailed as one of the most humane pieces of legislation this century.

The taxation-financed National Superannuation Scheme pays pensions to everyone at the age of 60, still working or not, the payments being indexed to national wage levels. Other state services indicate the extent to which New Zealanders have accepted sound welfare principles: a school dental service which gives free treatment by trained dental nurses to primary school pupils; free dental treatment by private practitioners to older children still at school; health camps for underprivileged children financed by the sale of government health stamps; free pharmaceutical products on doctors' prescriptions; payments to widows or other solo parents with children; payments to invalids. About one third of total central government spending goes on welfare payments, or around 10% of gross national product.

Outside the welfare field, New Zealand government has a stake in many areas. A state corporation was set up recently to help develop energy resources. The railway system is government-owned, as is the main domestic and overseas airline. The telephone system is government-owned. The state operates both television channels and the major national radio networks – indeed private radio broadcasting, taken over by the government in 1935, has only resumed in recent years, after a "pirate" offshore station broke the government monopoly.

Although there is a broad central government involvement in the life of New Zealanders, a parliamentary system modelled on England's and with similar constitutional conventions, a high quality civil service and an absence of corruption in public life maintain a sound democracy.

The closeness of central government to the people owes something to the miniature society which is New Zealand. A small population living in an uncrowded and generally prosperous country with modern public services of high standard are reasons enough for New Zealanders to feel that there are not too many countries which are better to live in. Theirs is by no means the wealthiest society on earth but the spread of wealth is comparatively even and the New Zealand invention of do-it-yourself has helped to keep it that way. No New Zealander regards himself as fully equipped for life's struggle unless he knows the skills of concrete-mixing, carpentry and house renovation.

It is no accident that more than a few New Zealand Prime Ministers – and many of their cabinet colleagues – have emphasised their debating points with hands grown strong on shovelling coal, building houses, driving bulldozers or working on the roads. Some would claim that they have been among the best Prime Ministers and Cabinet Ministers.

One of the magnificent sights which Auckland has to offer is its yachts in full flight on the Waitemata Harbour or Hauraki Gulf. Being the largest city in New Zealand, with more than a quarter of the total population, Auckland might be expected to be a showplace for the New Zealand boating and yachting passion and its fair climate lends itself to the sport. But one of the most impressive things is how many Aucklanders have built their own boats, many of a quality which any professional boatbuilder could envy. It is the same try-anything-once kiwi approach which has enabled so many New Zealanders to build a holiday home for themselves on the coast or around the lakes.

The outdoor life is basic to New Zealand leisure. For the more timid it may extend to no more than collecting firewood for the summer barbecue but it also ranges to the top of the exposed peaks of the Southern Alps.

Bush tramping and mountaineering, besides having given New Zealand the first conqueror of Everest, allows large numbers of city dwellers to get out into the open. There is plenty of open space to choose from and the narrow shape of New Zealand together with the extent of its mountains means that it is easy to reach the wilderness. Such easy access often disguises the real dangers which exist in the New Zealand bush. It is not uncommon in winter for trampers to become lost in heavy bush within just an hour's drive of the city and to have police and search and rescue teams out looking for them. Death from exposure or from mountaineering accidents makes an annual contribution to New Zealand's statistics.

Wild water rafting, too, has become a popular pastime in the great outdoors and the spread and sudden rise of New Zealand rivers under rain can make this hazardous. The short, steep rivers and their precipitous catchments mean rafters and trampers have to be watchful for changes in weather.

NEW VOYAGES OF DISCOVERY

The presence of so much high and rugged country in a place of New Zealand's size has influenced our literature and painting for a long time. The first artists who arrived here from England found it difficult to come to terms with the landscape. They painted volcanoes like Egmont and southern mountains like Mitre Peak with extreme exaggeration of their steepness. Heaphy's famous painting of Egmont suggests more a giant spire designed by a human eye than a mountain. The history of painting in New Zealand was virtually a history of landscape painting until the last 20 years and it mirrors a sense of human isolation in the midst of rugged country.

From the very first, landscape painters in New Zealand found a quality of light which brilliantly dressed a singular scene. Some recent painters have tried to convey the sharpness of the light by using dense colours or heavy, dark lines to border the meeting between land and sky or between different landforms.

If painters turned instinctively to the landscape, so did New Zealand writers. Katherine Mansfield caught the looming presence of the land in her stories and early novelists liked to accent human conflict by also setting human against landscape. Jane Mander typified this in *The Story of a New Zealand River*, which she located in the kauri forests and along the dark rivers of Northland where settlers were clearing the bush. Fiction set in urban communities – where the majority of New Zealanders have lived since almost the beginning of this century – is a new development.

Being gripped by the land, though, was natural to people who had largely come from the more placid shapes of Britain. In writing his novel *Man Alone*, Alan Mulgan spoke powerfully of the struggle of depression-hit farmers between the wars. But the enemy seems less the depression, than a dark land reluctant to yield up nourishment. This theme of "man alone" has been a recurring one in New Zealand writing, influencing not only serious literature but also lighter books which used the theme as the basis for a rough humour. It may be that New Zealand's almost complete lack of satirical literature owes itself to our concentration on the landscape – satire is born of town society.

Alan Mulgan's feeling for his country was a different attitude, grounded in New Zealand's own soil, from that of his father, who between the wars wrote a book called simply *Home*, a description of a pilgrimage back to Britain. It has a nostalgic, idealised sentiment far removed from the hard stare of Alan Mulgan at his own country. The two books are together a classic statement of the mental transition between colony and nation. Alan Mulgan wrote later that if New Zealanders forgot the country of their youth they would "wither internally of homesickness" – a warning about the flight abroad of many expatriates.

Novelist Robin Hyde said in 1938 that "in our generation we loved England still, but we ceased to be 'for ever England'. We became, for as long as we have a country, New Zealand."

Robin Hyde was speaking for all New Zealand when she wrote that. The Great Depression then receding had shown that mother England could not always be relied on to keep New Zealand's economy healthy by taking all the beef, mutton, lamb, wool, butter and cheese we could send her. New Zealand was still content then to rely on British diplomatic posts to represent her foreign policies abroad. In 1941, just three years after Robin Hyde spoke of a new national self-awareness, New Zealand established its first diplomatic post and in 1943 its own Department of External Affairs.

The country had shown a mood for independence before then. On Britain's declaration of war against Germany in 1939, the New Zealand Prime Minister had made a famous commitment to Britain: "where she goes, we go; where she stands, we stand". While New Zealand had no alternative, there was no doubt about her loyalty to Britain as the sun did finally begin to set over the British Empire.

However, Prime Minister Savage's patriotic statement was not the whole truth, for during those years leading to World War II New Zealand had disagreed often and bluntly with Britain over the need for collective action by the League of Nations against Fascism, Germany in Spain, Mussolini in Abyssinia. New Zealand, as Hyde noted, was shrugging off a cloak which for perhaps too long had obscured its vision of a world wider than either Britain or the Empire.

New Zealanders still believe they must make their own voyages of discovery overseas and the arrival of the jet age has enabled far more New Zealanders to travel than ever before. We produce more travellers for the size of our population than any other nation. Before the war, overseas travel by ship was slow and expensive and if fewer people travelled abroad then, perhaps more stayed away for ever, making their mark in many fields from editing prestige British dictionaries to going on stage. Many still do become expatriates, finding that their talents are not sufficiently well paid in a small country. This has been particularly true in the arts, for government subsidies to opera, ballet, theatre and music here are not massive.

A more complete urban society has grown up here since the war. New Zealanders now find it easier to satisfy their social needs. Travel has diminished the provincial smugness which used to be one of our less endearing characteristics and the growing number of tourists and businessmen coming here has helped broaden our views. There are still differences which impress themselves on visitors: there is an old Australian joke about the visitor who could not get into New Zealand at the weekend because it was closed. The 6 p.m. closing time for hotel bars which helped to form that attitude has changed to 10 p.m. and this has helped stimulate the entertainment scene. The recent introduction of Saturday shopping and a much more diverse variety of shops have given New Zealand a brighter public face.

The shops still remain mainly closed on Sundays except for the local "dairy", a kind of mixed, small, grocery-milkbar-icecream-confectionery-tobacco-bread shop which dots almost every street corner in every town, city and village. There are plenty of pubs, the larger cities have many excellent restaurants, good New Zealand wines appear on our tables, the water supply is safe and the country is given a regular wash and polish by the lively weather.

It there is a certain even tenor in the pattern of New Zealand urban life, it is probably because the New Zealand search for social and economic equality has been successful in guaranteeing a good life for most people. The demand for individual freedom has in a sense influenced New Zealand's path towards equality. As Bellamy had written, inequality destroys liberty, and New Zealanders listened hard to things like that. There is a widely-held belief that too much money at one end of society's scale will mean too little freedom at the other.

The reaction of new settlers against old rules was typified by Samuel Parnell, a 29-year-old London carpenter who in 1840 landed at Petone Beach, Wellington, and refused to work more than eight hours a day for a fellow-immigrant who offered him a job of building a store. The employer gave in. In 1849, Dunedin employers considered applying the "good old Scottish rule" of 10 hours work a day but the workers held out for eight hours and won. In 1899 Parliament enshrined the eight-hour day in legislation.

As one traveller in New Zealand once said: "Here Jack is not only as good as his master but indeed a good deal better!"

One of the interesting results of that opinion is that New Zealand's cities and towns tend to have a fairly similar life style, very much based on detached houses set in lawns and gardens. Yet there are some characteristics which dwellers in different cities like to offer as their own individual contribution to national life. Auckland has its two harbours and a unique collection of extinct volcanic cones which add visual drama to its setting. Its suburbs spread furthest and it comes closest to the concept of a large metropolis offering a range of entertainments. Even so, its central business district remains based on the single main street like the great majority of provincial towns.

Wellington, also sited on a superb harbour, has climbed up and over steep hills in a way which creates interesting streets of precarious-looking houses. It has a sort of crooked, hilly charm which many Wellington people say makes it the most intriguing city. Wholesale redevelopment of the harbourside inner area has given it a sparkling, modern appearance.

Christchurch celebrates an unusual degree of flatness by having beautiful gardens and parks. It can claim some of the best city architecture in the country, set off by the Avon River which meanders through it. Dunedin, in the far south where New Zealand's economic growth began with the 19th-century goldrushes in Otago, has a sturdy, old Victorian air which reflects its settlement by Scots.

Less than half New Zealand's population lives in these four main centres, which by comparison with developed countries overseas are modest in size and leisurely in the pace of life. Almost 70% of New Zealanders live in just these cities and 19 provincial centres where life is even more relaxed. Many visitors find it pleasant to come across towns which remind them of less hectic, former days in their own countries.

Farms and forests are still the main repository of New Zealand's wealth but during the last few years more intensive development of natural gas fields, one of them offshore from Mt Egmont, and of associated petrochemical industries has been occurring. Expansion of a steel plant which uses North Island west coast ironsands, an oil refinery and an aluminium smelter are adding heavily to New Zealand's industrial investment. The paddocks of green Taranaki around Egmont now sprout the towers and tanks of new energy projects besides grass for dairying. Yet grassland farming, forestry and a horticultural industry which is rapidly diversifying and expanding will continue for a long time to be New Zealand's main export producers.

Tourism is one of the fastest-growing industries in New Zealand and may be the best investment New Zealand can make in its future economy. No country is more ideal in which to promote tourism. Affluent in terms of temperate climate, spectacular mountains, lakes and rivers, unique forests and rich farmland and volcanic and thermal activity, New Zealand packs a big tourist package into a small space. Travel in New Zealand is easy, with good roads, modern, regular ferries between North and South Islands, efficient airlines and extensive bus and train services. There is always

something changing in the landscape passing by. The coastlines of these islands are both dramatic and beautiful, with many golden beaches and fine bays and harbours. And in a country where roads must climb high, many of the main highways are natural scenic routes – the Haast Pass, Arthurs Pass and Lewis Pass crossings of the Southern Alps, the main highway across the Central Volcanic Plateau, the coastal drive around the East Cape region, the roads through the National Parks and many others.

New Zealanders are ever-friendly and willing to share their country with visitors. There is plenty to go around. Sport includes some of the best trout fishing in the world – one of the imports which has been an unqualified success – and good game-fishing which has produced plenty of world records. Hunting, tramping, climbing, boating, skiing and just lying around soaking in natural hot pools are among the attractions, and if you play golf you will find in New Zealand the most scenic courses anywhere, readily available for play at a reasonable cost.

Bathed in the clean, fresh, bright air of the South Pacific, New Zealand turns a shining face to the heavens. There is discovery to be made here around every corner of the beckoning road. In a land of so much scenic magnificence it could scarcely be otherwise.

Previous page a beautiful sunset over the unusual Z-shaped Lake Wakatipu which, although 84 km long, is only 5 km wide. *Above* a view of Whangarei Harbour from the slopes of Mount Manaia and *facing page* Whangarei at dusk. Whangarei is the centre of the Northland Region of North Island; with a population of 40,000 it is also the region's largest city.

Above the beautiful land surrounding Matauri Bay is typical of much of pastoral New Zealand. Ninety Mile Beach, seen *facing page* at sunset, stretches away to the north of Kaitaia. This unbroken sweep of white sand is, in fact, 64 miles long. It is along this beach that the famed *toheroa* shellfish is found in abundance.

Facing page **some of the magnificent scenery along the road from Leigh to Pakiri.**
The Waipoua Kauri Forest *above,* **in the North Island, is one of the few extensive stands of mature**
kauri **left. The park contains 2,500 hectares of these giant trees, which may stand 50 metres tall**
and be nearly 2,000 years old. The timber of this slow-growing tree is highly prized and the
planting of rickers, young *kauri,* **is being encouraged in many areas of Northland.**

Auckland, seen *these pages* from Devonport across Waitemata Harbour, is by far the largest city in the country, with a population of some 800,000. The narrow isthmus was once heavily populated by Maoris descended from the *Tainui* canoe, but the aggressive behaviour of their chief, Kiwi Tamaki, in the eighteenth century brought down such a storm of *utu*, or revenge killings, that the area was virtually deserted when the first *pakeha* settlers arrived in 1840.

Queen Street *above* **is one of the most popular shopping streets in the city of Auckland.**
North of the Manukau Harbour Entrance can be found the surf-pounded west coast, which is
frequented by the citizens of Auckland. Piha is one of the most popular of the resorts; the
great Lion Rock *facing page***, which dominates the coast, can be climbed along a steep path, but**
only by the fit.

Living in such close proximity to the sea, the people of Auckland have far more interest in boats and the sea than most. It seems that anyone who can afford to buy and moor a yacht, launch or other pleasure craft, does so. Westhaven Marina *these pages* is a mute witness to the Aucklanders' love of 'messing about in boats'.

The Auckland Harbour Bridge *above and facing page* is glimpsed in any
view of the harbour. After thirty years of planning and controversy,
the 1,020-metre-long steel structure carried its first vehicle in
1959. Because of the growth of population on the North Shore, the
bridge was widened from 4 to 8 lanes in 1969.

Auckland's bustling city centre is well known as a magnificent shopping area. Customs Street *facing page* is lined with shops, but the endless stream of traffic is something of a problem for pedestrians. The Downtown Centre *above* is clear of road traffic and shoppers can wander as they wish.

Sheltering the waters of Hauraki Gulf from the open Pacific, the Coromandel Peninsula reaches out into the waters north of Thames. Mercury Bay *below* was so named because it was here that *HMS Endeavour* was anchored when Captain Cook observed the transit of the planet Mercury. Hahei Beach *facing page*, which is dominated by the remains of four *pa*, Maori fortified villages, is a favourite spot for skindivers.

The **Black Jack Scenic Reserve** *below*, near Kuaotuna, contains some of the most beautiful landscape of the Coromandel Peninsula. The nearby Black Jack Hill produces quartz crystals, sinter and pseudomorphs. The mist-shrouded **Firth of Thames** *facing page*, which lies off the other side of the peninsula, was so named because Captain Cook felt that the mouth of the Waihou River resembled that of the Thames. Though the Waihou is no longer known as the Thames, the Firth perpetuates the name.

Snuggled beneath the towering bulk of 395-metre-tall Pukewhakataratara lie the rich fishing waters of Wilsons Bay *below*. Despite the abundance of fish, they play a remarkably small part in the national economy; sheep, which graze the rich grasslands *facing page* are perhaps the single most important resource.

Of all the thermal sites around Rotorua, where hot springs and gases reach the surface, perhaps the most famous is Whakarewarewa *these pages*. Pohutu *above*, whose name means splashing, may spurt to a height of 30 metres and remain active for hours at a time. Likewise, it may remain dormant for hours, its activity heralded by the spouting of the Prince of Wales Feathers – a smaller nearby geyser.

The geothermal activity around Rotorua, apart from pervading the whole area with a sulphurous smell, produces many curiosities. One is found in the Waiotapu area *above*; the Lady Knox Geyser will erupt from its pool only when the water surface is covered by a film of soap. This strange phenomenon was discovererd by convicts doing the prison laundry. *Facing page* a hot pool at Whakarewarewa.

The town of Rotorua itself began life as a spa town after the Maori Wars had ended. The conscious use of mock-Tudor architecture, as at Tudor Towers *facing page*, was an attempt to recreate the atmosphere of a European spa town. The volcano of Tarawera *above* was thought to be long extinct until it erupted without warning in 1886. Sixteen thousand square kilometres of land were strewn with ash and rock and many roads, bridges and villages destroyed; but perhaps the most tragic result was the destruction of the beautiful pink and white silica terraces.

The steaming cliffs of Waimangu *below* testify to the instability of an area that has been wracked by volcanic eruptions many times in recent years. In 1917 an eruption destroyed a tourist hostel and the cauldron left behind is now filled by a 4-hectare lake of boiling water. The scalding waters of the area are too hot for fish, but ideal for the growth of algae *facing page*.

The size of the Waipa wood mill *below* is an indication of the importance of the timber industry to the Rotorua region. The Ohau Channel *facing page* carries water from Lake Rotorua, in the foreground, to Lake Rotoiti beyond. The lake was once a link in the canoe route to Rotorua, the canoes being portaged from Lake Rotoehu. Today, Lake Rotoiti is more famous as a rich trout fishing ground.

Cape Kidnappers *these page* marks the southern extremity of Hawke Bay. It was named by
Captain Cook after a canoe of Maoris first of all made off with some red cloth and
then tried to kidnap Taiata, a ship's boy who was sitting in the main chains. The
crew of *HMS Endeavour* opened fire on the canoe and in the ensuing confusion Taiata
managed to escape and swim back to the ship.

The beautiful sweep of the Bay of Plenty is epitomised at Ocean Beach *above*, where Mount Maunganui rises above the sea mist. *Facing page* the sun sets behind the mountains above Hastings. According to Maori myth the giant Te Mata was given the task of eating these hills before he could marry the girl of his heart. Not surprisingly he choked on one particular mouthful and fell dead, his body forming the peak that bears his name.

The Tuki-Tuki Homestead *below* is typical of the kind of elegant building that sprang up across the country after the Maori Wars. Opotiki *facing page* has today a population of some two and a half thousand, but during the days of the Hauhau Movement it was an isolated mission station. In 1865 the missionary, Rev Carl Volkner, was captured by Hauhauists. As part of their ceremony the Maoris hacked off Volkner's head and ritually drank his blood.

The rich land around Gisborne *these pages* is some of the best in New Zealand for market gardening, and the residents make full use of the combination of fertility and climate. Before 1874 Gisborne was known as Turanga. In that year the town raised a large sum of money to build a courthouse and gaol, only to see the government mistakenly spend the money on facilities for Tauranga, further north. The name change was soon approved.

Just off the East Cape Road, some 64 kilometres north of Gisborne, lies beautiful
Anaura Bay *these pages*. The marvellous stretch of golden sand and the rugged beauty
of the surrounding area make Anaura a great tourist draw. Captain Cook tried to fill
his water casks here, but the pounding surf hindered his boats and he moved further
south to Tolaga Bay.

Gannets usually nest on remote, rocky islands where they and their eggs will be safe
from predators. Cape Kidnappers *these pages* houses the only mainland breeding colony of
gannets in the world. The first birds appear in late July and the last leave in
March. Throughout these months the cape is a mass of screaming, squawking sea birds.

After naming Poverty Bay because he did not find any supplies there, Captain Cook sailed round East Cape to find a great sweeping bay running westward. Along this coast he found prosperous Maori villages and was able to reprovision *HMS Endeavour*, naming the area the Bay of Plenty. *Facing page* a scene from near the mouth of the Hawai River and *above* Okitu Beach.

Marking the eastern end of the Bay of Plenty *above* is Cape Runaway *facing page*. As
HMS Endeavour rounded the cape, five war canoes filled with Maori warriors put out to
intercept the ship. Captain Cook ordered his cannon to fire over the heads of the
Maoris; a display which so frightened the warriors that they were forced to 'run
away'. In this way Captain Cook named yet another coastal feature.

Hawke Bay *above* lies to the south of the Gisborne Plains *facing page*, beyond the
Mahia Peninsula. For many years the hills surrounding the east coast town of Gisborne
meant that it was only accessible by sea. Even today, the town is only linked with
the rest of the country by four roads and the atmosphere of isolation remains.

The mountains of the Tongariro National Park were *tapu*, or taboo, to the Tuwharetoa tribe, but in 1887 the tribe gave the peaks to the nation as a National Park. The symmetrical cone of Ngauruhoe *facing page* is the country's most active volcano, while Ruapehu, seen in the distance *facing page*, has a crater lake *above* which was only discovered in 1879 when George Beetham became the first man to climb the peak.

The population of hoofed animals is about twenty-five times the total number of human New Zealanders; a proportion unmatched anywhere else in the world. Such pastoral products as wool, meat and butter remain the nation's most important products, accounting for about fifty per cent of all exports. Farming activities shown are at Mahia Peninsula *below* and near Hastings *facing page*.

Below a tranquil Lake Taupo, with the snow-capped peaks of Tongariro National Park in the background.
Facing page the positioning of Great Barrier Island and the Coromandel Peninsula, means that the Hauraki Gulf is protected from all but northerly winds; a fact well appreciated by the Maoris, *hauraki* meaning 'north wind'.

Nestling beneath the slopes of Ruapehu is the magnificent, first class Chateau Tongariro hotel *below*. On the other side of Ngauruhoe is Lake Taupo *facing page*. Covering almost 620 square kilometres, the lake is not only perfect for sailing, but is also a superb fishing ground, where three-kilogram trout are a common catch.

The Waikato River *below*, which flows out of Lake Taupo near Nukuhau, has a flow which is carefully controlled by man and which is utilised for hydro-electric power. The lushness of this landscape north of Lake Taupo contrasts with the arid scene *facing page* to the south of the lake, where Ngauruhoe looms over the landscape.

Above the verdant slopes of the Taranaki Region, *above* near Toko, rises the majestic bulk of Mount Egmont *facing page*. The nearly circular Egmont National Park includes hundreds of hectares of native bush; remnants of the dense greenery that once covered the whole of the Taranaki Region.

The towering mass of Mount Egmont *these pages* dominates New Plymouth *below*. The rich soil of the region has been formed from the ash and rock thrown out from the volcanic mountain. Mount Egmont has not erupted since the arrival of the *pakeha*, but it did erupt about AD 1630, and some think that it may do so again.

Typical of the pastoral scenes so common on the grasslands are these from Hadfield Farm which lies near Paraparaumu, north of Wellington. The nation's exports of wool are currently around 300 million kilograms. Though most of this is exported raw, the wool processing industry is rapidly gaining ground.

The capital city of Wellington *these pages* was founded by the New Zealand Company in late 1839. For some time the centre of the growing settlement was a prefabricated, two-storied building which stood on the site of Lambton Quay *above*. This building was originally intended as a school, but soon became the hotel, the courthouse, the council chambers, the ballroom and the main cultural centre of the region.

For a quarter of a century after the town was founded, the growing population of Wellington *these pages* agitated and put out propaganda because the official capital of Auckland was remote from the principal centres of population and industry. Today, the cities' roles have changed and Auckland is the larger city, while Wellington is the capital city. Basin Reserve *facing page* is home of Wellington cricket.

In 1866 the citizens of Wellington built themselves a temporary wooden cathedral to serve until they had time to build a permanent church. It was to be a century before the new cathedral was actually built. During that time Old St Paul's *below* was repaired and altered many times, but today the interior is much as it was originally planned by the Rev. Frederick Thatcher all those years ago.

The coastal scenery of New Zealand is among the most varied and lovely in the world. It reflects the range of formation of the interior in its gentle slopes, *above* at Picton Harbour, and rocky outcrops *facing page*.

The South Island, according to the Maui cycle of legends, was the canoe in which Maui and his brothers fished when he caught his great fish, *Te Ika a Maui*, which became the North Island. The Kaikoura Peninsula *facing page* is said to have been the bench on which Maui braced himself when he hooked the fish. *Above* Queen Charlotte Sound.

It was from tranquil Sandy Bay *facing page* that the marble was shipped to Wellington for the construction of the Parliament Buildings. Picton *above*, on Queen Charlotte Sound, is the terminal for the rail ferry across the Cook Strait and is always busy with small yachts and pleasure craft.

Lake Tekapo *facing page* is just one of several morainic lakes in the Mackenzie Country, west of Timaru. The level of water in the lake is controlled by a cunningly concealed dam, which appears to be no more than a road bridge. *Above* a beautiful sunrise over Port Lyttelton, as seen from Summit Road.

The cattle raised on the Erewhon Station *facing page* and on the grasslands of South Canterbury *above* have helped to make New Zealand one of the world's leading exporters of meat and dairy products. In fact, over 300,000 tonnes of butter and cheese and 500,000 tonnes of beef are shipped abroad each year.

The Canterbury Plains are rich with grasslands and trees *facing page*, but inland, beyond Fairlie, lie the wilder lands around Lake Pukaki *above*. The lake, like so many in the area, was formed by glacial action many thousands of years ago.

Above **Lake Sarah and** *facing page* **Lake Pukaki. The particular milky-blue colour, so often seen in these mountain lakes, is due to their glacial origins. The ice of the glaciers grinds the rock to powder and the meltwaters carry this dust down to the lakes, where it remains suspended, giving the peculiar tinge to the waters.**

The Mount Hutt Range *above* contains one of the country's newest and most popular skiing resorts. Lake Pearson *facing page* is justly famous for its trout fishing, the fish having been introduced from Tasmania, where they had been introduced from Britain some years earlier.

The beautiful River Avon *above* meanders through the grid-like plan of Christchurch streets with no regard for neatness. *Facing page* Cathedral Square is a focal point for the whole of Christchurch, the lack of traffic gives a relaxed atmosphere, while the cathedral itself, which took some forty years to complete, provides a place for peace and prayer amid the bustle of city life.

These pages the Franz Josef Glacier is a popular place for tourists who can take long walks to see the spectacular scenery of the area. *Facing page* hikers crossing the Fletcher Bridge. The glacier itself is subject to great variations in size, melting and being added to in cycles that may last several years, but the general trend seems to be one of retreat.

Though, today, the terminals of the two great glaciers of the Southern Alps only descend to an altitude of 300 metres, a mere 14,000 years ago they reached the sea near Bruce Bay *facing page*. The retreat of the glaciers, which is a worldwide phenomenon, has left behind it deep U-shaped valleys, *above* at the foot of the Franz Josef Glacier.

The mighty Fox Glacier *facing page* is not only fed directly by snowfall on the névé but also by the Albert, Jewel, Abel Jansen and Explorer glaciers high in the Southern Alps. As the glaciers advance down the valleys they melt and their waters flow down to the sea; *above* can be seen a waterfall formed by meltwater from the Franz Josef Glacier.

The retreat of the glaciers to the Southern Alps has left behind many glacial features. One of these is Lake Matheson *facing page* which is a kettle lake – formed when blocks of subterranean ice, once buried beneath the glaciers, melt causing the soil above to collapse and form a depression that fills with water. *Above* is seen Hokitika Beach.

Bruce Bay *above* was once the centre of a violent riot by 3,000 enraged diggers who had forced the famous prospector, Albert Hunt, to lead them to his claim, only to find themselves abandoned in dense and unfamiliar forest. Important features of the west coast near Punakaiki are the layered limestone stacks *facing page* which the sea has carved into beautiful and fantastic shapes.

According to Maori legend Lake Hawea *above* has a magical floating island, which once carried the family of Ruia to a rich and plentiful land. Further north along the Haast Pass Road is the Makarora Valley *facing page* which provides rich grazing land in the shadow of the towering Young Range.

Only two species of mammal are native to New Zealand, both of them bats, but man has introduced many more. The Maori brought dogs and rats, but it was the *pakeha* that introduced the majority. Animals were introduced for many reasons; some, such as the sheep *facing page*, for farming and profit while others, such as the deer *above*, for sport.

The Remarkables *these pages* stretch away to the south of Queenstown in Otago, towering over the valley of Lake Wakatipu. Visitors with more stamina than most can make the tiring ascent of these 2,000-metre mountains, though it is recommended that a whole day be set aside for the attempt.

The Shotover River *above* flows down from Lochnager into Lake Wakatipu *facing page*. A combination of wind and water movements results in the unusual seiche which can raise the level in one part of the lake while lowering it in another. The Maoris ascribed this motion to the beating of a giant's heart which was submerged in the lake when the giant was burned to death by a jealous man.

Draining water from the Remarkables *facing page*, and from many hundreds of square kilometres of South Island, is the Clutha River *above*. On its upper reaches, near the Old Man Range, is the important hydro-electric power station at Roxburgh. Utilising the mass of water pouring down from the mountains in spring and summer, the dam produces electricity for use throughout the nation.

Though only 80 kilometres from the west coast, Queenstown *facing page* is many road kilometres from the sea. The motorist must either travel north, by way of Lake Hawea and over the Haast Pass, or along the shores of Lake Te Anau and through the Homer Tunnel. A view from the latter route is shown *above*. The tunnel was begun in 1932 to help ease the unemployment problem and three men were killed during construction.

Near to Queenstown, on the shores of Lake Wakatipu, stand the mighty Remarkables *facing page* and the reconstructed gold mining village of Golden Terrace *above*. At the village the buildings and atmosphere of the 1860s are recreated for the visitor.

Otago Harbour *above* is the stretch of water protected by Otago Peninsula and has, at its head, the 'Edinburgh of the South'; Dunedin. The harbour is well known for its abundant bird life, among them penguins, shags and oystercatchers, but perhaps the most sought after, and least seen, are the albatrosses.

The two chief cities of Otago Harbour, Dunedin *above* and Port Chalmers *facing page*, have a long and close connection. The original Dunedin settlers first landed at Port Chalmers and the two towns have similar industries and interests.

Glendhu Bay *above* is one of the most tranquil spots on the shores of Lake Wanaka. The beaches offer wonderful views across the lake and Mount Aspiring can be seen some 10 kilometres to the west. The Otago Peninsula *facing page* stretches north-eastwards for over 20 kilometres from the town of Dunedin, and includes both beautiful scenery and rich farmland.

The Otago region covers much of southern South Island and contains a remarkable diversity of landscape. The land around Roxburgh is rich enough to support large areas of orchard *above*, indeed, the town is dominated by the orchards and their associated industries. The land around the Kakanui Mountains *facing page* is less productive.

Otago Harbour *above* **is a stretch of sheltered water which lies behind the Otago Peninsula, north of Dunedin. On the other side of the peninsula is the wild and spectacular coast of Sandfly Bay** *facing page.*

Mount Cook National Park *these pages* stands high in the Southern Alps and contains some of the best mountain scenery in the world. Many of the rugged, snow-capped peaks top the 3,000-metre mark and offer among the most challenging climbs in the country. One of the most awe-inspiring wonders in the park is the mighty Tasman Glacier *above*, whose meltwaters flow into Lake Pukaki.

The Southern Alps *these pages* include the towering bulk of Mount Cook, seen *facing page* reflected in the waters of Lake Pukaki. It was the race to conquer this peak in the 1880s and '90s, more than anything else, that started the New Zealand interest in mountaineering that was to culminate in Sir Edmund Hillary's conquest of Mount Everest in 1953.

Apart from the mountaineers' huts scattered amongst the peaks and glaciers of Mount
Cook National Park *facing page*, the only accommodation in the area is the Tourist
Hotel Corporation's Hermitage *above*, which is built on the site of an earlier
structure which burnt down in 1957.

The staggering scenery of Mount Cook National Park, the Tasman Glacier *above* and *facing page* **Mount Cook, is the result of titanic earth movements which began about a hundred million years ago. The jagged peaks so formed have been more recently shaped by the advance and retreat of the glaciers which have gouged out deep valleys and shattered the peaks.**

The beautiful rivers and streams of New Zealand reflect the diversity of landscape and climate of the country. In the highlands *above* the water flows swiftly over a bed of bare rocks, but in the lusher lowlands *facing page* the flow of the stream is impeded by the growth of plants and fallen trees.

New Zealand is famed not only for the quality of its meat but also for that of its
wool. The sheep *above* near Hastings show just how productive a single animal can be.
In many parts of the world the horse *facing page* has outlived its usefulness to man,
but in the pastoral parts of New Zealand it is still indispensable to the stockman.

The tumbling waters of the Poerua River *facing page* eventually flow into the Grey River. The bare stretches of shingle along the banks show the high level of the river when it is full of melted snow after the spring thaw. *Above* brooding clouds lower over the foothills of the Southern Alps.

The rolling terrain of the Otago Peninsula *above* on the east coast, contrasts strongly with the rugged, rocky terrain to be found on the west coast near Knights Point *facing page*. The different formations are due to the varied geology of the regions.

Taken from Titi Koraki on the Otago Peninsula, the view of Victory Beach *above* shows, in the foreground, the tidal entrance to Papanui Inlet. Further south on the same peninsula is the nature reserve of Sandfly Bay *facing page*, where the Lion Rock stands just offshore.

The important Southland port of Bluff *above* is in a natural harbour, sheltered from all directions. The amount of frozen meat and processed aluminium being exported through the port has increased in recent years and the town's future seems assured. At Curio Bay *facing page* the stumps of petrified trees, the remains of a 150 million-year-old forest, can be glimpsed amid the surf and seaweed.

The true power of prehistoric glaciers is not fully realised until one sees the spectacular cliffs of Fiordland, as at Milford Sound *facing page*. The plunging, vertical valleys were gouged from the virgin rock by the relentless grinding of the rivers of ice. *Above* are the Mirror Lakes in a similar, though smaller glacial valley on the road from Milford to Te Anau.

The road to Milford Sound runs along the valley of the Eglinton River *above* for many kilometres, before climbing into the mountains beyond Lake Fergus towards the Homer Tunnel. Waterfalls, like the Bowen in Milford Sound *facing page* are formed when streams reach the precipitous edge of glacial valleys and throw their water to the valley floor far below.

Ever present in the landscapes of western Southland are the majestic mountains that break the horizon with their jagged profiles. *Above* can be seen the River Waiau, which flows from Lake Te Anau to Lake Manapouri and thence to the sea at Te Waewae Bay. The lush pasture land *facing page* is near Lake Hauroko, whose waters also drain into Te Waewae Bay.

Plying the waters of Milford Sound, taking visitors on pleasure cruises, is the *Mitre Peak 2*, which is named after the imposing conical mountain which towers above the sound and is seen shrouded in mist *facing page*. The Maoris came to the sound in search of greenstone, but the climate and lack of soil deterred them from founding any form of permanent settlement.

Stewart Island *these pages* is largely untouched by human hand; there are, for instance, barely 30 kilometres of road on the island. The timber industry, once so important to the island, has largely ceased and the peaceful atmosphere is only shattered by the day-trippers who come from the mainland to view the island. *Overleaf* Dog Island, five kilometres off the Southland coast.